Dedicated to Carol Sibley and Sarah Smedman,
two professors who shared their love of children's literature with me in Minnesota.

Teaching With Picture Books
in the Middle School

Iris McClellan Tiedt
Minnesota State University at Moorhead
Moorhead, Minnesota, USA

INTERNATIONAL
Reading
Association

800 Barksdale Road, PO Box 8139
Newark, Delaware 19714-8139, USA
www.reading.org

The International Reading Association attempts, through its publications, to provide a forum for a wide spectrum of opinions on reading. This policy permits divergent viewpoints without implying the endorsement of the Association.

Director of Publications   Joan M. Irwin
Editorial Director, Books and Special Projects   Matthew W. Baker
Special Projects Editor   Tori Mello Bachman
Permissions Editor   Janet S. Parrack
Associate Editor   Jeanine K. McGann
Production Editor   Shannon Benner
Editorial Assistant   Pamela McComas
Publications Coordinator   Beth Doughty
Production Department Manager   Iona Sauscermen
Art Director   Boni Nash
Senior Electronic Publishing Specialist   Anette Schütz-Ruff
Electronic Publishing Specialist   Cheryl J. Strum
Electronic Publishing Assistant   John W. Cain

Credits   Illustration, page 78   Benjamin M. Baker

Library of Congress Cataloging in Publication Data
Tiedt, Iris M.
    Teaching with picture books in the middle school/Iris McClellan Tiedt.
        p.   cm.
    Includes bibliographical references (p.) and index.
    ISBN 0-87207-273-8
    1. Picture books for children–Educational aspects–United States.   2. Middle school teaching–United States.   I. Title.
        LB1044.9.P49   T54   2000   00-058129
        373.133'5–dc21

Contents

To the Reader...

I am pleased to share this book about using picture books to stimulate students' thinking with teachers who are looking for ways to enhance their teaching. My aim is to show you how much picture books have to offer students in the upper grades, including middle school and even high school students.

Picture books are fascinating. Some are incredibly beautiful. Some relate stories that are charming or funny or surprising. Some are classic works. These illustrated books are almost always delightful to read, especially when reading to someone else who can share your enjoyment.

Picture books provide wonderful opportunities for classroom discussion. The authors have chosen an amazing diversity of concepts to introduce in these attractive short books—problem solving, living in earlier times, fighting wars, immigrating to new lands, getting along together, and more. The topics presented invite students to think and to respond.

In addition to subject matter to consider, picture books provide engaging models for writing. Pattern books, short narrative forms such as fables and pourquoi tales, autobiographies, and poetry are among the variety of beautifully illustrated books that suggest kinds of writing that older students will find challenging.

Older students also will enjoy reaching out to younger children by sharing picture books with them. Students can polish their oral language skills as they practice reading aloud, dramatizing, or storytelling as ways of opening books for beginning readers. And, older students can write and illustrate original books designed for children, thereby stimulating their own creativity.

In this book I have endeavored to introduce middle school teachers, and adult readers in general, to the wonderful possibilities of the picture book. My focus is on using these books as instructional resources. Throughout this text I suggest various methods for engaging older students with specific books, and I present many teaching suggestions to support teachers' efforts, including fully developed, reproducible lesson plans in Appendix A. Browse through the chapters and explore this exciting approach to teaching.

Iris M. Tiedt

There is no frigate like a book
    To take us lands away,
Nor any coursers like a page
    Of prancing poetry.

This traverse may the poorest take
    Without oppress of toll;
How frugal is the chariot
    That bears a human soul!

Emily Dickinson

Illustration by Sydney Roark from *Stuartship* by Ryan Collay and Joanne Dubrow. Reprinted by permission of FlowerPress Books, Box 2217, Eugene, OR 97402.

CHAPTER 1

Using Pictures Books in the Middle School to Stimulate Thinking

Using picture books in the middle school–does that surprise you? We usually consider picture books appropriate only for the elementary school classroom. Classified as "easy books," they are housed in the children's section of the library where middle school students never see them. We need to take another look at these so-called "little" books because picture books frequently present complex ideas that are suitable for use with older students. Some middle school teachers have discovered that the picture book can be an exciting teaching tool that involves their sixth, seventh, and eighth graders in meaningful learning experiences.

Authors of picture book fiction typically are experienced storytellers, sharing humorous tales, folklore, and adventure. Their language tends to be clear and often beautiful. In addition, these books are illustrated by talented artists who not only contribute to the beauty of a book, but also amplify the information presented.

Each picture book, whether fiction or nonfiction, offers a distinctive contribution that you can use to enhance your teaching. My purpose in writing this book is to help you explore the possibilities for using picture books to stimulate thinking, speaking, listening, reading, writing, and media literacy in your classroom. You will discover narratives that teach a lesson as well as books that provide exciting information about all kinds of subjects that cross the curriculum. Picture books introduce students to people of different cultures from around the world; they provide interesting perspectives of the history and geography of our planet. The illustrations add a dimension to reading that books for adult readers usually do not have.

The Advantages of Using Picture Books

The picture book is an efficient way to introduce a topic to a middle school class. You need to find only one copy of the book you want to present, and you can read most of these books aloud to a class in 15 to 20 minutes. Thus, in a short time the whole class is prepared to respond to something they all know.

Although it was not the authors' primary intent, each skillful picture book writer has prepared a well-written text that you can use to add interest to your teaching. For example, Paul Goble creates handsomely illustrated books about Native American life; Patricia Polacco tells stories about Italian Americans. From fables to poetry to biographies—thousands of titles are available to meet your classroom needs.

Moreover, middle school students enjoy these attractive books. They are pleased to encounter familiar titles that they perhaps read with their parents as young children, such as *Cinderella* by various authors, *The Little Engine That Could* by Watty Piper, or *The Story of Babar, the Little Elephant* by Jean De Brunhoff. And, even advanced students are intrigued by the clear presentation of sophisticated ideas written by authors such as Dr. Seuss, Ed Young, or Eve Bunting. Some picture books also offer special support for students who are learning English as a second language. Remember, too, that thousands of books are published each year that are new to today's middle school students.

If you need further convincing or the support of a strong rationale for using picture books to help you teach more effectively in the middle school, just review the following list (Tiedt & Tiedt, 1999). Picture books can help you

- present part of our literary heritage.
- model intonation and the pleasure of reading.
- stimulate student writing.
- introduce oral language activities.
- present provocative topics that stimulate thinking.
- lend fun to learning and teaching.
- develop rapport with students and a sense of community.
- teach grammar and style.
- explain interesting information about different cultures.

- expose students to varied literary genres.
- suggest creative art activities.
- introduce extended thematic studies.

Despite all I can say here, only reading some of the truly delightful books that are available will fully convince you of their value. The books and their illustrations must sell themselves.

Defining the Picture Book as a Category

In general the picture book contains illustrations that are almost as important as the text in conveying meaning. Most people equate the picture book with the preschool and elementary-grade classroom. However, books that are categorized as picture books vary widely.

Usually, we think of picture books as books that contain simple text dealing with universal themes that children can understand. The illustrations are appropriate to this text and suitable for the young readers for whom the book is intended. These books are wonderful read-alouds for young children, and they are natural selections for the beginning reader. Examples of this type of picture book include *The Snowy Day* by Ezra Jack Keats and *Make Way for Ducklings* by Robert McCloskey. Although the storyline of these books is not complex, they still may be useful in middle school as material that the older students will read aloud to children in earlier grades or as models for creating original picture books. These books also can be used to study and admire the artwork and perhaps to compare the color and pattern used by Keats with the black line drawings by McCloskey.

Another group of picture books is composed almost entirely of pictures with little or no printed text. Commonly called "wordless books," these books are great to stimulate storytelling and language development. Particularly good for young children are those books with a simple humorous plot, for instance, Mercer Mayer's *Frog, Where Are You?*, although middle school students will enjoy these, too. Some wordless books are not useful in the primary grades at all, but are wonderful for generating both oral and written stories at the middle school or secondary level. One such example is *The Mysteries of Harris Burdick*, written and illustrated by Chris Van Allsburg. The intriguing illustrations in this book are excellent Story Starters (writing prompts) especially effective with older students.

Still other picture books present complex concepts that are more appropriate for advanced readers. For example, there are impressively illustrated informational books that are much too advanced for primary-grade children. Many middle schoolers will pore over the detailed illustrations in a book such as *Horses: History, Behavior, Breeds, Riding, Jumping* by Jackie Budd. Another fine picture book that offers exciting ideas following a theme appropriate for middle school is *Talking Walls*, written by Margy Burns Knight and illustrated by Anne Sibley O'Brien. I explore such books in Chapter 7.

A final group of picture books is those that need to be used with care. Although I do not condone censorship, certain picture books contain material that is far too mature to be considered for instructional purposes in the middle school. Such a book is Maya Angelou's *Now Sheba Sings the Song*, illustrated handsomely by Tom Feelings. Feelings has drawn numerous beautiful charcoal sketches of black women from different parts of the world, and Angelou has written lovely poetry to accompany them. However, Angelou's sexual references and the nudity in some pictures would make me hesitate to share the book in a middle school classroom. On the other hand, sharing selected passages and some illustrations, perhaps on a transparency or an enlarged copy in a display, usually permissible for classroom use, might enhance a study of the contributions of African Americans. My purpose in pointing out this kind of book is to emphasize the need to preview any material that you share with your students. I do not include such books in the chapters that follow because there are many other fine books that are less likely to create controversy with parents.

Enjoy the wealth of picture books that is available. Used wisely, they will help you present many thought-provoking lessons in your middle school classroom.

Overcoming Possible Resistance to Teaching With Picture Books

Although I know that picture books have much to offer the middle school teacher, I still recognize the fact that some students, and even parents, may question your use of these books in the middle school. Therefore, let's consider ways of answering parental questions and overcoming student resistance.

First, picture books should not dominate your instruction. Most of the time your students will be studying age- and ability-appropriate textbooks and literature. However, you can use picture books occasionally as a means to an end, for example, as a model for writing a biographical sketch or painting a mural. In presenting these books you never even mention "picture book," but simply share an example of writing by one author or the kind of art used by one talented person who in this case illustrated a book for young people.

At times, a study could focus directly on picture books, for example, if all students were creating books to share with younger students, a challenging writing and art project. You would provide many picture books that students could examine, thereby learning how to evaluate books and illustrations and how to write and illustrate a story for younger readers. In this case the objective for examining picture books is understandable, and students are clearly learning age-appropriate skills. No one is likely to protest such use of this literary form.

Second, your attitude in presenting a picture book to your class is what often will determine whether use of a picture book is accepted by the class. If you have developed a positive classroom climate and rapport with your students, you usually can share an interesting book you have discovered. After students listen to the book and see the illustrations, then you can ask a leading question to involve them with the topic presented. Or, you might introduce a funny book you can say "someone gave you," for example, Fred Gwynne's *A Chocolate Moose for Dinner*. Then, challenge students to think of other examples of comical plays on words. To involve students further, ask for two or three volunteers to find more books by this author. Students are likely to respond positively to such overtures from a trusted teacher.

Third, sometimes you really don't need to *show* a picture book to the class. For instance, if you want students to write the form of poetry *haiku*, you might use transparencies to present two poems, illustrated beautifully by Ezra Jack Keats, from Richard Lewis's *In a Spring Garden*. Later, after talking about this poetry form and writing original poems, the students can examine the whole book and others as models for presenting their own poetry. At other times you simply may duplicate a poem, fable, or whole story so that you can read from printed sheets to present content you want students to hear. Thus, you avoid the connection with a book for young children if you think that will be a problem for your students.

Fourth, the secret to avoiding student resistance to a picture book is either to open the book for them, as in reading it aloud yourself for some clear purpose, or to give students an acceptable reason to read the book. These young people who are trying to grow out of childhood into young adulthood are not likely to open a picture book voluntarily. You need to legitimatize in some way their reading a primary-grade book. For example, cross-age tutoring that engages middle school students in reading with young children can be seen as a service activity.

The delighted response of the younger students to these older friends will reward the middle schoolers amply for their efforts in selecting great picture books to read together. If your middle school students keep logs that record their experiences with the young learners, they can share in small groups in your classroom what they discover about children and their reactions to reading and school.

Finally, parents usually have little reason to question the use of picture books unless you appear to overdo it. They are concerned that their children are learning, moving perhaps beyond their age level, so they may worry about what may seem like activities that do not challenge their students' intellect. Therefore, if you plan a study of folklore, for example, that will involve students in reading several illustrated children's books, explain to parents the purpose of this study and some of the objectives to be achieved. (You might send an information sheet home regularly to parents to let them know some of the upcoming learning activities that you will be featuring in your classroom.) Perhaps you can invite their support, in this case, asking if they have an interesting folk tale to share in person or on tape.

If you have a clear sense of what you aim to achieve through the use of picture books, you should have little difficulty with parents' questions. And if you care about students and their welfare, and you show it, most students will be happy to join you in the kinds of learning activities that picture books support.

Getting Started

How do you begin to use picture books in the classroom? In this section I will show you how and where to find effective picture books and how to plan lessons around them.

Exploring the Possibilities

First of all, you need to know a variety of picture books. *Teaching With Picture Books in the Middle School* is designed to introduce you to a wide variety of books that you can integrate into your curriculum. After reading this first chapter, which sets the stage for a program that makes full use of these delightful picture books, feel free to select other chapters that promise to meet your needs. If your specialty is the language arts, look at the chapters on oral language skills, reading, and writing. If you teach science or math, turn to the chapter on subjects that cross the curriculum, remembering, of course, that all the language arts skills are important to learning in your classroom, too. Browsing through the Contents and the Index are other ways of discovering topics that especially fit your concerns.

This book, however, is merely an introduction to the possibilities for using picture books to stimulate learning in the middle school. Your local public library is a rich resource that you will want to explore. Let the children's librarian know of your interest in picture books that you can use with older students. He or she will be pleased to locate titles that seem appropriate and to share new books that may be useful for the studies you plan. Find out what kinds of resources are available that focus on picture books—books, recorded materials, filmed presentations, or Internet connections. Ask the librarian to point out the picture book section and resource books about children's literature. Ask, too, if the library has any lists of recommended picture books. For example, each year outstanding art in children's books is recognized by the American Library Association with an award named in honor of the 19th-century English illustrator Randolph J. Caldecott. Many Caldecott Award books will be discussed in later chapters of this text, and a full list of these titles is included in Appendix B. Just to get a feel for illustrated books, you might begin by locating a few of the following classic books, all illustrated by the author:

Sam, Bangs & Moonshine by Evaline Ness

The Story of Babar, the Little Elephant by Jean De Brunhoff

Where the Wild Things Are by Maurice Sendak

Crow Boy by Taro Yashima

Don't forget about the nonfiction books in the children's section. You may be amazed to see the many illustrated books that deal with a variety of topics—animals, geology, history, diverse cultures, language, and so on.

Also visit a bookstore that carries a good selection of children's books. Spend an hour or so browsing through the picture books to see what the store has to offer. You probably will find a few books that are so engaging that you will want to buy them for your personal collection!

Cooperative Planning of Lessons Around Picture Books

The most effective way of developing lessons that use picture books for teaching in the middle school is to work with a team. Ask two or more interested teachers if they would be willing to explore picture books with you and to share their findings. Just think of the results if three of you were to spend several hours in the public library compared to what you could do alone. Besides, it's more fun if you can share your enthusiasm, and it helps if several of you explain to a colleague what you are doing and why.

You might begin by showing *Teaching With Picture Books in the Middle School* and a few of the picture books recommended in it to some of your friends. Here are a few especially attractive books that you might look for, guaranteed to please almost any teacher and to suggest immediate uses in the classroom:

Why Mosquitoes Buzz in People's Ears, written by Verna Aardema and illustrated by Leo and Diane Dillon (Caldecott Award winner)

The Girl Who Loved Wild Horses by Paul Goble (Caldecott Award winner)

The Wave, written by Margaret Hodges and illustrated by Blair Lent (Caldecott Honor book)

Book, written by George Ella Lyon and illustrated by Peter Catalanotto

Arrow to the Sun: A Pueblo Indian Tale by Gerald McDermott (Caldecott Award winner)

Tar Beach, written and illustrated by Faith Ringgold

When I Was Young in the Mountains, written by Cynthia Rylant and illustrated by Diane Goode

Owl Moon, written by Jane Yolen and illustrated by John Schoenherr

All of these books are written beautifully and contain outstanding artwork. After reading each one, consider how you might use the book in your classroom. As mentioned, each year thousands of new picture books are published. Remember, however, that many wonderful books were published long ago, so don't equate "new" with "the best." Your local public library will contain many great picture books that may be out of print, but even some of the early books, often considered classics, continue being printed. Examples include *And to Think That I Saw It on Mulberry Street* by Dr. Seuss and *Madeline* by Ludwig Bemelmans.

Planning Effective Lessons

Following is a simple lesson plan form that I use for the lessons referred to throughout this book, which are in Appendix A. This form can be used for planning a one-period activity, or it can be adapted to plan a project that extends

Thinking + Lesson Plan Form

Title of Lesson: _____

Expected Outcomes
The learner will

    1. _____

    2. _____

    3. _____

Teaching/Learning Strategy

Resources:

Directions

    Step I:

    Step II:

    Step III:

Assessment Performance

    1.

    2.

over a week or more. You might like to duplicate the blank form to use as you and your colleagues create lessons on your own. Or, you can scan the form into your computer and enlarge it to fit your needs. The lesson plans in Appendix A may be reproduced for classroom use.

This form is intended to guide you in completing a lesson or project plan that focuses on encouraging students to think, compare, evaluate, summarize, and synthesize, but note that the title begins with *Thinking +*. The + sign indicates that this activity is designed so that students will begin to think about a stimulus that they have observed or have experienced through their other senses, for example, hearing, smelling, tasting, or touching. The + sign also indicates that feelings can be included, the emotions that are often ignored or even excluded from the middle school classroom.

Remember, too, that middle school students, as is true of students of all ages, need variety and a change of pace during their school experiences. Lectures and silent reading have their place, but do insert stimulating oral strategies such as dramatization and ensemble speaking or reading aloud as ways of responding to literature. Humanities approaches that integrate literature, history, art, and music into middle school studies also will enliven the curriculum and make it more meaningful. Interactive group studies are particularly effective in the middle school. Throughout the book I suggest using cooperative learning groups or CLGs for various learning activities.

Students need to be fully engaged if real learning is to take place. Specific ways of designing "Thinking +" lessons and projects will be described in detail throughout this book. Examine the lesson plan based on the content of a picture book that focuses on the topic of conservation or stewardship: Thinking + Lesson Plan 1 in Appendix A (see page 142; see also the illustration that opens this chapter). Notice that this lesson crosses the curriculum to integrate science and the language arts.

The Organization of This Book

I have grouped ideas for using picture books with middle school students under eight chapter titles plus two appendixes:

- Sharing Our Literary Heritage

- Promoting Reading Development

- Stimulating Thinking, Talking, and Writing

- Extending Student Knowledge About Language and Literature
- Understanding and Appreciating Diversity
- Crossing the Curriculum
- Stimulating Creativity
- Introducing Thematic Studies
- Appendix A: Lesson Plans
- Appendix B: Exploring Further

Each of the eight chapters focuses on one specific aspect of instruction. Sample lesson plans in Appendix A, stimulating instructional strategies, and annotated lists of books are included to suggest picture books that will enhance your teaching in varied ways. Throughout this book I have tried to offer teaching methods that integrate the language arts and reading across the curriculum.

Appendix B contains ideas and additional resources that you can explore as you continue to develop a repertoire of engaging learning activities to share with your students. Thousands of picture books now sit on library shelves just waiting for you to open them!

Conclusion

In this introductory chapter we have explored the possibilities for using picture books to enhance teaching in middle school classrooms. I have presented a strong rationale for sharing attractive picture books with middle school students while at the same time acknowledging the kinds of resistance that teachers might meet from students or parents. As a way of helping you get started with using picture books, I presented a sample lesson plan to show you how a lesson might be developed using a specific book. And, I have encouraged you to work cooperatively with your colleagues in order to lighten the task of finding appropriate books and creating lessons. In Chapter 2 we will continue our exploration by introducing students to literature that is part of our common heritage—Mother Goose rhymes and nursery tales.

Old Mother Goose, when
She wanted to wander,
Would ride through the air
On a very fine gander.

From Grover, E.O. (Ed.). (1997). *Mother Goose: The original Volland edition* (F. Richardson, Ill.). New York: Checkerboard Press.

CHAPTER 2

Sharing Our Literary Heritage

Do you recognize such names as Simple Simon, Humpty Dumpty, Little Boy Blue, and Mary, Mary, Quite Contrary? "Of course," you say, "They're Mother Goose rhymes." And perhaps you can recite the verses from memory:

Little Boy Blue,
Come blow your horn.
The sheep's in the meadow;
The cow's in the corn.

But, where is the little boy
Who looks after the sheep?
He's under the haystack
Fast asleep!

Such verses are learned in younger years as the stories are read aloud to children by adoring parents and grandparents. Because this is what may have happened to you, you may assume that most children have had similar experiences.

But, do you really think that all of your seventh graders know these Mother Goose characters? Can they chant these intriguing old rhymes? Would they understand the humor in a comic strip that referred to Old King Cole or "Hickory, Dickory, Dock; The mouse ran up the clock"? And how about the nursery tales *The Three Little Pigs* and *Jack and the Beanstalk*? Or, consider other familiar fairy tales such as *Rumpelstiltskin, Cinderella, Little Red Riding Hood,* and *The Emperor's New Clothes.* Do your students know these stories?

Let's look at our students' lives realistically. Working parents may be too busy or too tired to spend much time reading aloud to their children in the evenings. Also, we need to remember that our students come from increasingly diverse cultural backgrounds. So, we cannot assume that all middle school students and even their parents or caregivers will know Mother Goose and nursery tales that are primarily of European origins.

It behooves us, therefore, to find out just what our students do know about this literature that many of us share. If Mother Goose is totally unfamiliar and many students have never heard of *The Three Little Pigs,* then perhaps we have a responsibility to introduce this literature to them before they begin high school. Their chances of being introduced to these rhymes and nursery tales will be less and less likely as they advance in school.

Following are suggestions for assessing student knowledge and introducing Mother Goose, nursery tales, and other familiar folk tales to students in the middle school. Issues related to diversity are addressed only briefly in this chapter because this topic is so important that a full chapter is devoted later to multicultural picture books, including poetry and folklore.

Engaging Students With Mother Goose

Start with a focus on Mother Goose rhymes because the rhymes are brief and the total body of literature is fairly well defined. Begin with an assessment of students' knowledge and then engage them in activities designed to expand their acquaintance with verses such as "Hey, Diddle, Diddle," "Jack Sprat," and "Mary Had a Little Lamb."

Getting Organized

Obtain several collections of Mother Goose rhymes. Some recommended editions include the following:

Mother Goose's Words of Wit and Wisdom: A Book of Months, compiled by Tedd Arnold. This is an attractive collection with unusual cross-stitched illustrations.

A Child's Treasury of Nursery Rhymes, compiled by Kady MacDonald Denton. This is an oversized book with humorous illustrations.

Tomie dePaola's Mother Goose, compiled and illustrated by Tomie dePaola. This book contains colorful, childlike art.

The Glorious Mother Goose, compiled by Cooper Edens. This compilation contains art by traditional illustrators from the early 20th century. It also suggests an interesting study for gifted students or others on early illustrations in children's books.

Twinkle, Twinkle: An Animal Lover's Mother Goose, compiled by Bobbi Fabian. This book has full-page presentations of each verse facing a full-page illustration.

The Random House Book of Mother Goose: A Treasury of 306 Timeless Nursery Rhymes, compiled and illustrated by Arnold Lobel. Lobel's compilation contains attractive, humorous illustrations. See also *The Arnold Lobel Book of Mother Goose: A Treasury of More Than 300 Classic Nursery Rhymes*.

Brian Wildsmith's Mother Goose: A Collection of Nursery Rhymes compiled and illustrated by Brian Wildsmith. This collection has outstanding art.

An especially good hardbound collection that you can usually find at local bookstores is *Mother Goose: The Original Volland Edition*, edited by Eulalie Osgood Grover and illustrated by Frederick Richardson. The illustrations, many of which are full sized, are attractive and presented in an appropriately quaint style. (See the example on page 16.) This would be a good collection to own as a reference book.

Read through the rhymes yourself, noting some of the more familiar ones, such as the following:

Baa, Baa, Black Sheep

Humpty Dumpty

Jack and Jill

Little Bo-Peep

Little Boy Blue

Little Jack Horner

Little Miss Muffet

Old King Cole

Old Mother Hubbard

Peter, Peter Pumpkin Eater

The Queen of Hearts

Simple Simon

Sing a Song of Sixpence

Three Blind Mice

Because these rhymes have been passed down orally, you may find slightly different versions of each one, so use the version you feel most comfortable with. Remember that students, too, may have learned different versions.

Also, begin collecting cartoons or comic strips that refer to Mother Goose rhymes or other such lore. These comics are fun and will help you show students one reason for knowing this literary heritage we share. For example, the creator of the comic strip "Mutts," Patrick McDonnell, recently showed the dog reading "The Three Little Kittens" aloud to the cat. When the three good little kittens find their mittens and receive some pie at the end of the verse, both the cat and dog are happy. Then, the weary dog says, "And *that's* the *last* time!" Clearly, he has read the poem many times. The cat jumps up and down, shouting, "Again! Again!" obviously not tired at all of having the verse repeated.

Assessing Student Knowledge of Mother Goose Rhymes

Present the following assessment activity as a game. Although you will collect the results of this "quickie quiz" to guide your teaching, make it clear that student scores have nothing to do with grades you assign. You might discuss your interest in knowing whether children today are learning the humorous chants and jingles that you learned as a child, saying, for example, "Sometimes we teachers assume that students have learned things at home or in the early school years that they really have not."

As you begin this assessment activity, explain to students that you will give the first line of a verse and that you want them to supply the second line, if they can. If they do not know the verse, they will simply leave that answer blank.

Work with two sample items orally first, so that students understand what is expected. For example, read aloud the line "Mary had a little lamb." Then, ask how many students can supply the next line, and have someone tell you what it is ("Its fleece was white as snow"). A second example might be "Pussy Cat, Pussy Cat, where have you been?" Students should supply the next line, "I've been to London to visit the queen."

Give each student a copy of the quiz that follows on the next page. State again that you predict that a few students will know all the verses, others will know some of the verses, and some students will know none of the verses. That is what you want to find out, so you know how to plan your teaching. Read aloud each item on the quiz, pausing to allow students to write the second line, if they know it.

What's the Next Line?
Quickie Quiz on Mother Goose Rhymes

1. Simple Simon met a pieman

   _____

2. Jack and Jill went up the hill

   _____

3. Hickory Dickory Dock

   _____

4. Mary, Mary, quite contrary

   _____

5. There was an old woman

   _____

6. Little Jack Horner

   _____

7. Three blind mice, three blind mice,

   _____

8. Old Mother Hubbard

   _____

9. Jack be nimble

   _____

10. Peter, Peter, Pumpkin Eater

   _____

Collect the students' papers and score them later. Noting the results for each student, use the results to plan future lessons and to guide class grouping for activities relating to Mother Goose rhymes.

Answers to the quiz
1. Going to the fair.
2. To fetch a pail of water.
3. The mouse ran up the clock.
4. How does your garden grow?
5. Who lived in a shoe.
6. Sat in a corner.
7. See how they run.
8. Went to the cupboard (to get her poor dog a bone).
9. Jack be quick.
10. Had a wife and couldn't keep her.

Follow this quiz with the activities described in the following pages. For students to become familiar with Mother Goose rhymes, they have to read them or hear them a number of times. Plan activities that will engage all students with these rhymes periodically over several weeks.

Who Was Mother Goose?

Introduce the study of Mother Goose rhymes by telling students something about Mother Goose and the origins of these rhymes. There are various stories about the identity of a person called Mother Goose. The history of these verses and how they came to be published is presented in detail in the Volland collection recommended earlier. One thing is certain: In 1697 Charles Perrault published a collection titled *Contes de Ma Mere L'Oye* or *Tales of My Mother Goose.* Explain that we usually read these rhymes to young children who love to repeat them and learn to say them from memory. Because many people living in the United States know these rhymes, we often see or hear references to the content of the poems in the newspaper or in conversations.

Reading Rhymes Aloud

Each day read aloud a few Mother Goose rhymes. Ask the students to join with you as you slowly repeat one of the shorter rhymes, for instance, "Jack and

Jill." (In any class, it is likely that at least a few of the students will know some of these poems.)

Using large type on your computer, make copies of rhymes that can be transferred to transparencies or duplicated for students to use. One day after reading several verses aloud, display a full-page transparency of, perhaps, "Peter, Peter, Pumpkin Eater." Here are the lines to this verse:

> Peter, Peter, pumpkin eater
> Had a wife and couldn't keep her.
> He put her in a pumpkin shell
> And there he kept her very well.

Have the class read the verse aloud together. Then, ask them to clap in time as they repeat the poem again. (Most of these verses have a pronounced rhythm that lends itself to chanting.) Some students may develop creative raps based on one or more of these rhymes.

Acting Out Rhymes

Divide the class into cooperative learning groups of four or five students. Give each group a copy of one of the rhymes to read together. Their task is to dramatize the rhyme and present it to the class. "Little Miss Muffet," for example, can be quite dramatic with the spider swooping down to sit on the tuffet as Miss Muffet scurries away in fright.

Members of the presenting group may chant the lines of the poem together, or a chorus may be composed of other students in the class. Keep the emphasis on having fun with these activities. After the class has developed these dramatizations, you can arrange for them to present their program to a kindergarten or first-grade class. This is also an effective presentation for a Parent Teacher Association meeting or a meeting of another local organization.

Singing the Rhymes

Some Mother Goose rhymes have been set to music and sung over the years. You may introduce the tunes to the class. (Ask for help from the school's music teacher or a talented student.) Musical interpretations can be added to the students' presentations. Students who play the guitar or other instruments can share their abilities. The melody commonly used for "Mary Had a Little Lamb" is shown on the next page. Illustrated by Tomie dePaola, *Mary Had a Little Lamb* includes the music and all the verses written in the 24-line poem attributed to Sarah Josepha Hale circa 1830. If you cannot find music for a rhyme, invite students to create an original melody.

Artistic Interpretations of Rhymes

One simple activity is to give each student a copy of 1 of the 10 Mother Goose rhymes featured in the quickie quiz. Have each student read the rhyme silently. (Be available to provide help, as needed.) Then provide colored pencils, crayons, or paints so that each person can illustrate the rhyme as he or she envisions the action described. Have students sign their art and sort the rhymes into two or three volumes for later use. Students may create an illustrated collection of Mother Goose rhymes to place in the school library. Remember that such creative activities should not be limited to children in the elementary grades. If all students use the same size poster board on which to display an illustrated verse, the posters can be bound to create a Big Book to share with kindergarten children and first graders who are learning to read.

Some students might be challenged to use computer art to display their verses. If you are skilled with computers, you might guide students to develop an impressive multimedia presentation perhaps titled "Mother Goose on the Loose!" This program could be shared with other classes or groups of parents at an open house.

Reading Lessons for English-as-a-Second-Language Learners or Slower Readers

Knowing Mother Goose rhymes is important for all students. However, the repetition and rhyming make some Mother Goose verses especially good material for developing reading skills. In Appendix A, Thinking + Lesson Plan 2 (see page 143) is a lesson plan designed for students for whom English is a second language.

Repeat the Thinking + Lesson Plan 2 with other Mother Goose rhymes, for example, "Humpty Dumpty" or "Simple Simon."

Gifted middle school students could prepare the materials needed for this lesson. They could teach such lessons providing good experience in organizing and presenting learning materials. These students might form a club called Junior Teachers or Teaching Assistants.

Mary Had a Little Lamb

Old Tune

1.   Ma – ry   had   a   lit – tle   lamb,
2. It   fol – lowed her   to   school   one   day,

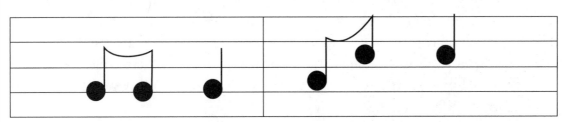

lit – tle   lamb,   lit – tle   lamb.
school one   day,   school   one   day.

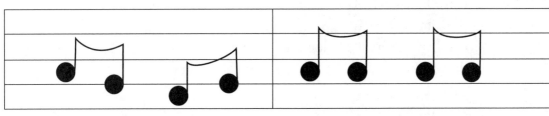

   Ma – ry   had   a   lit – tle   lamb, its
It fol – lowed her   to   school   one   day, which

fleece was   white   as   snow.
was   a–   gainst the   rule.

Reading Nursery Tales and Other Familiar Folk Tales

Another category of children's literature that is commonly introduced to pre-schoolers is the nursery tale. In this chapter I will focus on familiar nursery tales such as *The Three Little Pigs* and *Goldilocks and the Three Bears*. *Cinderella* is included here, but fables and other folklore will be presented in later chapters.

Assessment Activity

Again, begin with an assessment activity, presenting it as a game. Let students know that you simply want to find out if they know these stories. Reproduce the quiz on the next page so that each student has a copy. Read aloud each item in the quiz slowly, repeating it twice so students have a chance to think. Reading the items aloud ensures that reading ability does not influence the results. If students know these stories, the clues should be sufficient to tell them which plot is summarized in each item. Give students time to write each title, and tell them that correct spelling is not necessary.

Answers to the quiz
1. Little Red Riding Hood
2. Three Billy Goats Gruff
3. The Little Red Hen
4. The Three Bears; Goldilocks and the Three Bears
5. Henny Penny; Chicken Little; The Sky Is Falling
6. Cinderella
7. Jack and the Beanstalk; Jack the Giant Killer
8. The Three Little Pigs (and the Big Bad Wolf)

Reading Tales Aloud

Begin reading aloud some of the popular nursery tales, perhaps one or two each week, depending on how you want to develop this unit of study. Two useful collections of these tales are *Eric Carle's Treasury of Classic Stories for Children*, compiled and illustrated by Eric Carle, and *The Three Little Pigs and Other Favorite Nursery Stories*, compiled by Charlotte Voake. Often these tales have been presented as an individual story in a book illustrated by a noted artist. Suggested titles are listed in the following discussion.

What's the Title?
Quickie Quiz on Nursery Tales

1. Little girl, basket of food, grandmother, wicked wolf

   _____

2. A little goat, a middle-sized goat, a big goat, a troll

   _____

3. A hen, grains of wheat, a dog and cat, homemade bread

   _____

4. A blonde girl, three bears, three chairs, three beds, porridge

   _____

5. An acorn, sky, a chicken, Cocky Locky, Foxy Woxy

   _____

6. A pretty girl, two bad sisters, fairy godmother, glass slipper

   _____

7. A boy named Jack, beans, a giant, treasures

   _____

8. Three pigs, three houses, a bad wolf

   _____

I recommend your reading the stories aloud yourself rather than having a student read. The rapport developed as you read to the class is important in maintaining student interest. Also, many teachable moments will occur as you read aloud. Reading aloud while students listen has many other advantages that we sometimes forget. Even middle school students learn much about language and about the reading act itself as they listen. They are hearing examples of varied grammatical structures. In addition, they learn concepts such as the following:

1. Reading is very enjoyable.
2. A plot has a beginning, a middle, and an end.
3. Authors paint a picture in words that you can visualize.
4. Writers use many interesting words.

Following the reading of a story, for example, *Jack and the Beanstalk*, have students take turns retelling the events that happen in this tale. An excellent presentation of this tale about Jack and the giant is retold and illustrated by Swiss artist John Howe. You might have a group retell the same story several times on different days as they recall the plot details.

The Voice Choir

Cumulative tales, for example, *The Gingerbread Boy*, are especially recommended for retelling in different ways. The repetition in the cumulative tale makes it easy for students to memorize and to chant together. Look for the 1975 edition by Paul Galdone, which has retained much of the original text. Students love repetitive language such as this:

Run! Run! Run!
Catch me if you can!
You can't catch me!
I'm the Gingerbread Boy,
I am! I am!

A newer edition of this tale that uses similar rhythmic language is the 1998 retelling by Jim Aylesworth, illustrated by Barbara McClintock.

The Gingerbread Boy lends itself to presentation as ensemble speaking, sometimes called a Voice Choir, in which the class recites the story together. Such oral language activities are highly recommended for middle school students. As in any choir, parts can be assigned with an occasional duet or solo voice. A small group of voices can supply the narrator's comments. After the class has mastered this story, have them present it to other classes or to a group of visiting parents. For help with such oral language methods, including Readers Theatre, which follows, see *Language Arts Activities for the Classroom* (Tiedt, P., Tiedt, I., & Tiedt, S., 2000).

A Readers Theatre Presentation

Readers Theatre, a method appropriate for young children as well as adults, is another excellent oral language activity that gives middle school students an opportunity to interact with a story they have heard or read. Planning and executing a presentation requires critical thinking skills such as comparison, evaluation, and synthesis. Teach students how to script a story and to present it orally, as described in Thinking + Lesson Plan 3 in Appendix A (see page 144).

For Thinking + Lesson Plan 3 have students bring in different versions of *Little Red Riding Hood.* Luciano Pavarotti has written an introduction to the one by famous Italian illustrator Beni Montresor. This artist chose to present the original story as Charles Perrault wrote it, so you can see the hapless Red Riding Hood inside the wolf's belly. John Goodall provides a fresh interpretation, casting the characters as animals with the little girl as a mouse and the woodsman as a bear; the wolf, of course, could only be a wolf! This book also has unusual cutaway pages that move the action along. After reading different versions have students discuss which one they like best and why.

Other stories that can be presented in similar fashion include *Chicken Little,* which is sometimes called *Henny Penny.* Sally Hobson presents a useful version of *Chicken Little,* which has attractive illustrations that students might try to emulate on a mural. H. Werner Zimmermann tells the story as *Henny Penny.* This version is especially recommended for English-as-a-second-language (ESL) students or students who need help with reading. The illustrations are delightfully funny.

Goldilocks and the Three Bears is another favorite tale that includes several roles. Look for the work of James Marshall who delights in adding humorous interpretations in his illustrations and in his retelling of the story. For example, he begins thus:

> Once there was a little girl called Goldilocks.
> "What a sweet child," said someone new in town.
> "That's what *you* think," said a neighbor.

Marshall portrays Goldilocks as a naughty young girl who does just as she pleases. Disobeying her mother, she takes a shortcut and goes into the home of the three bears. She messes up everything and finally falls asleep in the little bear's bed until the three bears return to their home.

Stories Associated With Music

Some nursery stories have been set to music. A classic example is *Hansel and Gretel*, with music by Engelbert Humperdinck. Check your teachers' resource center for a copy of this record and play the music. Have children act out this old story from the Brothers Grimm. Share some of these examples by different retellers and illustrators:

Hansel and Gretel, retold and illustrated by Anthony Browne. This version is an authentic retelling with quaint, appealing illustrations.

Hansel and Gretel, retold and illustrated by Susan Jeffers. Jeffers's version contains especially fine art, including some double-page spreads.

Hansel and Gretel, retold and illustrated by Jane Ray. This book has large full-page illustrations.

This story of abandonment, betrayal, and ultimately triumph offers interesting discussion material for middle school students. They might, for example, talk about the role of the stepmother, perhaps comparing the role in this story with that in *Cinderella* and other tales. An excellent journal entry might address the questions: Why is the stepmother always portrayed negatively? and Is this a fair representation?

Acting Out a Fairy Tale

Choose a favorite tale like *The Three Billy Goats Gruff* that has very clear, explicit roles as a first story for acting. A recommended version of this story is by Tim Arnold. The excellent pictures and clear language make it especially appropriate for slower readers or ESL students. Another version that is equally effective is by Paul Galdone. Remember that older editions may be out of print but are often in your public library.

Introduce this activity by first reading the tale aloud to the whole class. Then have the class discuss the various roles presented in the story, for example, Little Billy Goat Gruff, Middle-Sized Billy Goat Gruff, Big Billy Goat Gruff, and the Troll. Students can add roles, if they like, perhaps, passers-by on the road, commenting about the activity they observe, "I wonder why those goats keep crossing that little bridge?" Encourage students to be creative, remembering that these tales have been retold many times through the years. Also, they can choose to add repetition and rhyme for artistic effects. The roles of director and producer will be to help make decisions about such recommended changes.

Ask for volunteers to act out the story as students take turns retelling the story. Have different people try to act out each role, providing different interpretations of how each goat would walk. Those who are telling the story will reflect this walking as they say the words, "Trit-trot, Trit-trot," for each of the goats, beginning softly for the smallest goat and speaking very loudly and ferociously for the biggest goat. Body movement also will be appropriate.

This dramatization can be shared with students from the early grades. Follow this activity with a similar one in which groups of five students collaborate to present different stories.

Following Up With Media References

Even after you have completed a study of Mother Goose rhymes or fairy tales, you will often find occasion to mention the rhymes or tales to students during the school year. Encourage students to bring in references to the rhymes or nursery tales that they hear on television or read in the newspaper. It is amazing how many times we find references to the literature of childhood in daily newspapers, particularly in the comic section, and other media. We frequently allude to these characters from literature in our daily speech: "Don't be a dog in the manger" or "Sour grapes." Display the references and discuss them with the class to reinforce the relevance of studying rhymes and fairy tales.

Developing a study of Mother Goose rhymes and nursery tales is enjoyable for both teacher and students. Try it once and you will surely want to repeat it with other middle school students.

Conclusion

In this chapter we have delved into a rich resource, Mother Goose rhymes and nursery tales. These stories are part of our cultural heritage, and I have provided a rationale for introducing this literature to middle school students. Recognizing the need for giving students a valid reason for studying this "literature of childhood," I have suggested various ways of engaging older students with these verses and stories. I also have included sample lessons that address the needs of all students, including those for whom English is a second language. In Chapter 3 we will focus specifically on using picture books to support the development of reading abilities.

From *Frog Goes to Dinner* by Mercer Mayer, copyright ©1974 by Mercer Mayer. Used by permission of Dial Books for Young Readers, a division of Penguin Putnam Inc.

CHAPTER 3

Promoting Reading Development

The more you read,
the more you know.
The more you know,
the smarter you grow.
The smarter you grow,
the smarter your voice,
when speaking your mind
or making your choice.

National Library Week Poster

The focus in this chapter is on encouraging middle school students to read with ease and enjoyment. Because language abilities are foundational to successful reading, I begin this chapter with oral language activities and include ideas for engaging students with the reading process and guiding them to enjoy reading by sharing books with others.

Beginning With Oral Language

It is not uncommon for some students to pass through elementary school without becoming "hooked on books"; thus they never gain reading fluency and self-motivation to read. These reluctant readers need special support and successful experiences with language in the middle school. Oral language activities may provide the successful interaction with books that leads to independent reading.

"Reading" Wordless Books

Wordless books are nonthreatening fun. These picture books encourage students to use language by telling the story depicted in the illustrations. They also involve reluctant readers with books in a positive way. Working with wordless books can lead students to reading other picture books and, gradually, more age-appropriate literature. Wordless books also can be useful with ESL students.

Introduce students to *A Boy, a Dog, and a Frog*, the first of Mercer Mayer's books about a boy who owns a frog. They get into all kinds of mischief. Students will delight in "reading" this wordless book aloud, inventing the dialogue and description as they go along. Have them tape their stories, then they can write their individual stories to enter in a class book. Mayer's other titles about the boy and his frog include *Frog on His Own*; *Frog, Where Are You?*; *Frog Goes to Dinner*; and *A Boy, a Dog, a Frog, and a Friend.* (See the illustration on page 32.)

Some students might create wordless books to share with primary-grade children. This activity offers one way of providing a successful experience for students who love to draw, but are not particularly interested in reading. Of course, they need to plot the story to be told in pictures just as Mercer Mayer has so cleverly done. Other wordless books that you might locate and share with students include the following:

The Alphabet in Nature by Judy Feldman. This alphabet book introduces ideas about nature in the paintings that accompany each letter. Feldman wrote a similar book, *Shapes in Nature*, that introduces interesting concepts to talk about.

Do You Want to Be My Friend? by Eric Carle. Little Mouse is looking for a friend. On each page he finds a tail. As the page is turned, you see the owner of the tail, thus creating an intriguing pattern that middle school students might find challenging.

A Flying Saucer Full of Spaghetti by Fernando Krahn. In this book small elfin creatures play with a rich young girl who doesn't like spaghetti. They fly the spaghetti across town to a hungry child who is glad to get it. The pictured story provides interesting discussion for a group of students. After planning a possible plot, they could tape their story for sharing.

Time Flies by Eric Rohmann. This is a more sophisticated wordless book that appeals to all ages. In fine oil paintings this illustrator depicts a world of the past filled with dinosaurs and flying reptiles. The artist's work received the Caldecott Honor Book Award. Groups of students could generate possible Story Starters for each of these paintings.

The Mysteries of Harris Burdick by Chris Van Allsburg. Fourteen full-page drawings are accompanied with only a caption and a line of prose that suggests a possible story line in Van Allsburg's book. These intriguing drawings are perfect stimuli for oral or written stories at the middle school level. Students could work with one picture in a cooperative learning group as they compose a group story to share with the rest of the class.

Ask your librarian to help you find more of these entertaining books if they meet your students' needs.

Using a Listening Center

A listening center can be used effectively for learning activities that provide benefits for gifted students as well as those who need support in reading at the middle school level.

The gifted student. Talented students can tape stories that less able readers or beginning readers in the elementary grades can use to support their reading at the listening center. You can develop this activity along two lines:

1. A service project: This is an excellent service project for gifted students. After preparing one or more tapes, they can present them to a kindergarten or first grade class. They might consult with the teacher first to find out what books would be especially helpful.

2. Oral interpretation: Recording a story challenges students to prepare their oral interpretation with emphasis on clear enunciation, accurate pronunciation, and intonation. Their performances can be evaluated based on those criteria. Students who concentrate on performing well will produce more effective, useful tapes than will those who read with little expression.

Books that gifted students might choose to present to early readers are the following:

Rikki Tikki Tavi, the well-known story by Rudyard Kipling, illustrated in one edition by Jerry Pinkney.

Snow White and the Seven Dwarfs: A Tale From the Brothers Grimm translated by Randall Jarrell and illustrated by Nancy Ekholm Burkert. This book was named as an Honor Book for the Caldecott Award and is now available in paperback.

Mirette on the High Wire, written and illustrated by Emily Arnold McCully. This book won the Caldecott Award for its elegant paintings of 19th-century Paris.

Manuela's Gift, written by Kristyn Rehling Estes and illustrated by Claire Cotts. This story about a young Latina girl focuses on the love and understanding among family members.

Less able readers. Slower readers or ESL students benefit from reading a book supported by the spoken words on a tape prepared by gifted students, as described earlier. Selected picture books provide brief text that is appropriate for stimulating practice material. The student follows the written text as the voice provides the words. The student then tries to read along with the voice. The end result should be that he or she reads the book independently. This practice often enables a student to read a whole book for the first time. Here are several picture books to consider for this purpose:

Abuela, written by Arthur Dorros and illustrated by Elisa Kleven. A pleasant story illustrated with colorful collages that contains some Spanish words, which might be supportive of Hispanic students.

Princess Furball, retold by Charlotte Huck and illustrated by Anita Lobel. An interesting version of *Cinderella*, this tape can be used when the whole class is studying different versions of this familiar tale.

Brown Bear, Brown Bear, What Do You See?, written by Bill Martin Jr and illustrated by Eric Carle. A simple pattern book for beginners.

This House Is Made of Mud/Esta casa esta hecha de lodo, written by Ken Buchanan and illustrated by Libba Tracy. This book contains poetic prose in English and in Spanish; fine art complements the text.

Jewels, written by Belinda Rochelle and illustrated by Cornelius Van Wright and Ying-Hwa Hu. A story about an African American family that will have general appeal. The book emphasizes storytelling by grandparents who share with their grandchildren. It would be good for an intergenerational theme study, too.

Using prepared cassettes or compact discs (CDs). Another way of using the listening center is to play cassettes or CDs that often are tucked into the front cover of a picture book. Students of all ability levels can listen to these recorded stories. Gifted students might use the recordings as models for their own taping. Students who need support also might use these professionally prepared recordings to support their reading of the book. Two picture books that include recordings are as follows:

The Emperor's New Clothes: An All-Star Illustrated Retelling of the Classic Fairy Tale. Introduced by Steven Spielberg, this favorite Hans Christian Andersen tale is presented by a celebrity cast of known actors and a team of award-winning illustrators. All have donated their work to the Starbright Foundation, a charitable organization devoted to helping children who are seriously ill. The cast is introduced in order of appearance on the tape in a special section at the end of the book. This unique presentation includes a tape and the handsome oversized book.

Ira Sleeps Over by Bernard Waber. This favorite book is one that middle school students may know. It would be a good selection to share with young children.

Ask the librarian to suggest other cassettes and CDs of recorded books for your students.

Storytelling

Telling stories is a good way to engage student interest in reading and writing. Encourage students to share short anecdotes and jokes as a preliminary activity for storytelling. Then have them begin with short stories or talks. They can share their stories with one another as they prepare to share them with primary-grade children.

Patterned tales. Stories that follow a distinct pattern are easier for students to tell. Try some of the following:

Mouse, Look Out! by Judy Waite. A humorous story introduces an engaging refrain as the cat chases a mouse through an empty old house. Readers will join in: "Mouse, look out! There's a cat about!"

So Say the Little Monkeys by Nancy Van Laan. This author employs rhythm and repetition to tell a story based on a Brazilian folk tale about monkeys who want to play all day. This would be a good story to tell preschoolers.

Town Mouse and the Country Mouse by Jan Brett. This is a lovely rendition of an old fable. The illustrations of these cunning critters must surely be shared as the story is told.

Would They Love a Lion? by Kady MacDonald Denton. Kady wants to be a bird, then a bear, and so on until she decides to be a lion. This story invites acting out by young children who end up taking a nap!

Book talks. Students can tell what happens in a book in a short summary designed to interest other students in reading a book. For example, a student who has read the funny role reversal *Petronella* by Jay Williams might say something like this:

> In the tradition of all great fairy tales, there are three princes and the youngest prince always triumphs. King Peter and Queen Blossom are unhappy, therefore, when the third child turns out to be a girl! Petronella, as she is christened, has a mind of her own. When the older princes set out to seek their fortunes, she appears with her bag packed determined to find a prince! She finds a prince, a very unsatisfactory prince, so she brings home an enchanter instead.

A wonderful book to share with others is *Back Home*, written by Gloria Jean Pinkney and illustrated by her husband, Jerry Pinkney. In this warm family story a young African American girl, Ernestine, travels by train to visit her relatives who live on the family homestead in North Carolina. Her cousin, Jack, teases her, but they part friends. The author/illustrator team describes the rural culture and the family relationships nicely through words and pictures.

Students could prepare book talks for younger students. They will need to choose books designed to appeal to the children they plan to address.

Overcoming shyness. Many students are too shy to participate in storytelling activities at first. These students may appreciate the kind of book that tells about someone else who had similar problems. Bill Harley relates such a predicament in *Sarah's Story*. Illustrated imaginatively by Eve Aldridge, this book tells of Sarah's consternation when the teacher announces that everyone is going to tell a story because she has no story to share. What follows is a story that no one can top when Sarah explains what happened to her on the way to school.

Laura Simms tells the story of a shy first grader in *Rotten Teeth*, illustrated by David Catrow. Melissa needs something interesting to share for show and tell, so her helpful older brother suggests a bottle of old teeth found in their dad's dental office.

Before engaging in storytelling activities, students could discuss their own nervous feelings when expected to stand in front of the class for any purpose. Perhaps, they can share some methods to ease their fears.

Using a flannel board. Props like a flannel board make it easier for students to present a story to a group, especially for the first time. Middle school students can combine art with storytelling by making figures to mount on the board as they tell a story. For example, students might choose to tell little children a story that is just silly fun like *Swine Divine*, written by Jan Carr and illustrated by Robert Bender. Rosie the pig had a pretty good life eating swill and rolling in the mud as pigs like to do. Then, her owner decided she should "ham it up" for the photographer. When he dressed her in a tutu, Rosie had had enough. She tore out of the store and headed home for a mud bath. The pictures depicting Rosie's antics are marvelous!

Another funny narrative is *Is There Room on the Feather Bed?*, written by Libba Moore Gray and illustrated by Nadine Bernard Westcott. Here is a story about a farmer and his wife who have many different kinds of animals on the farm. One night during a terrible storm, the farmer and his wife lay snugly under a feather bed. They hear a tapping at the door, and they admit a duck and a goose who want to share the warm feather bed. One by one the animals come in to share the feather bed. Each time the farmer's wife welcomes them with the following:

"Why bless your hearts,
such a noise, such a fuss.
There's room on the feather bed
For all of us."

Finally, comes a voice calling:

"I'm a small plump skunk
who cannot swim.
I'm asking politely
May I please come in?"

The farmer's wife welcomes him, too, so all are piled on the feather bed. Suddenly, the other animals and the farmer, realizing who has joined them, leap out of bed and run outside. However, after getting thoroughly soaked, they decide to come back where they all have breakfast in bed together. This story is a delight to tell and retell with children joining in.

Middle school students might tell a third-grade class of Cassie Louise Lightfoot's dream as Faith Ringgold relates it in *Tar Beach*, a Caldecott Honor book. Ringgold is an outstanding artist specializing in story quilts, huge hangings that tell stories from her own life and from history. The "tar beach" is the rooftop where her family picnicked on a warm summer night, and Cassie dreamed of flying freely over Harlem. Figures from the story can be cut from colored felt to be placed on a flannel board in the order of their appearance.

Groups of two or three students might develop presentations together. Each group might choose a creation story from the 25 collected and retold by Virginia

Hamilton and illustrated by Barry Moser in *In the Beginning: Creation Stories From Around the World*, a Newbery Honor book. The author explains each myth at the end of the story. Drawn from many cultures, these stories represent diverse thinking from such groups as the Chinese, Native American tribes, Guineans, Christians, and so forth. Flannel board presentations based on these stories can be shared with another middle school class.

Opening Humorous Books for Reluctant Readers

Invite students who are not naturally motivated to read by introducing them to humorous books that make them laugh. Such books may lure them to turn the pages as they become interested in what else the author has to say.

Funny Ways With Language

The Amelia Bedelia books by Peggy Parish have long been favorites because they are so funny. Amelia, who is a maid, is always confusing the meanings of words, taking them literally. When her employer tells her, for example, to take out the spots in a polka-dotted dress, Amelia diligently cuts out all the spots rather than using stain remover. When Peggy Parish died, her nephew, Herman Parish, continued the Amelia books. The latest is *Amelia 4 Mayor*. Other titles by Herman Parish include *Bravo, Amelia Bedelia!* and *Good Driving, Amelia Bedelia*. The older titles by Peggy Parish can still be found in libraries.

Humorous books about teachers always have appeal. One example is *Miss Nelson Is Missing*, written by Harry Allard and illustrated by James Marshall, which tells the hilarious tale of a teacher who disguises herself as her own substitute. She gives the students such a bad time that they are delighted to see Miss Nelson when she returns as herself.

Another delightful story is Judy Finchler's *Miss Malarkey Won't Be in Today*, illustrated by Kevin O'Malley. This teacher envisions all the strange substitute teachers who might appear, for example, Ima Berpur—such silly fun!

Investigating Tall Tales

The humorous tall tale is peculiarly American. Present these stories with "tongue in cheek" as you share these spoofs that young people usually enjoy.

Students will delight in Johnny Appleseed's tale about his brother, Nathaniel. Andrew Glass wrote and illustrated *Folks Call Me Appleseed John*. He includes information about the real Johnny Appleseed, John Chapman, who also loved to tell stories like this tall tale. Set in French Creek in northwestern Pennsylvania, the story encourages students to use the maps that decorate both inside covers of the book to trace Johnny Appleseed's travels. Students will enjoy reading this story aloud and acting out the parts. Writing their own tall tales will be a natural follow-up to reading this book.

Another figure from American folklore might be introduced by reading *The Bunyans* by Audrey Wood. Wonderful illustrations by David Shannon enhance Wood's story about the mighty Paul's wife and two children. This book provides a great model for students for expanding a known story along creative new avenues.

These stories could motivate students to locate other tall tales about, for example, Pecos Bill and John Henry. American literature is full of such folk tales as the tall tale. Anne Isaacs, author, and Paul O. Zelinsky, illustrator, combine their talents to present *Swamp Angel*. This humorous tall tale from Tennessee features Angelica Longrider, a renown woodswoman, who saved a wagon train from Dejection Swamp, and introduces the gigantic bear Tarnation, with whom Longrider struggled. Students might compare this tale to those about Paul Bunyan.

In *John Henry*, Julius Lester bases his tale of an African American folk hero on the well-known ballad. Jerry Pinkney contributes beautiful art to complement the text. Another type of lore from the United States is regional, as in *Mary on Horseback: Three Mountain Stories*, retold by Rosemary Wells and illustrated by Peter McCarty, about a real person in the Appalachian area of the United States, Mary Breckinridge.

Carl Sandburg tells the story of *The Huckabuck Family and How They Raised Popcorn in Nebraska and Quit and Came Back*, illustrated by David Small. Pony Pony Huckabuck finds a silver buckle in a huge squash she is preparing to cook. When the family leaves Nebraska, they will not return until they see a sign. When Pony Pony finds a second silver buckle in another squash, they "reckon" that is sign enough, so they return to Nebraska.

Sharing Books With Others

The more students read the better they read. Our job as teachers often entails simply providing incentives for students to read. One incentive is scheduling middle school students to read books aloud twice a month to young children. The youngsters delight in having the "big kids" come to their classroom, and the older students are well rewarded by the attention of the little ones. Even slower readers will practice repeatedly reading a picture book to do a good job in an elementary school room. Thus, their fluency and reading comprehension improve over the months as does their motivation to read.

Books about animals are popular with children, especially those that humanize the animals. Many old favorites are in the library. *Bedtime for Frances*, written by Russell Hoban and illustrated by Garth Williams, tells about a little badger who does not want to go to bed. *Owl at Home*, written and illustrated by Arnold Lobel, pictures an owl who lives in a cunning, well-furnished home. *Lyle, Lyle, Crocodile*, written and illustrated by Bernard Waber, features a crocodile that eats dinner with a human family. The classic tale *The Story of Babar, the Little Elephant*, written and illustrated by Jean De Brunhoff, depicts animals of all kinds dressed in human clothing as they have adventures.

Lois Ehlert writes and illustrates attractive books about animals, for example, *Top Cat*. In this book she relates the familiar story of an older cat that has to get along with a new kitten that suddenly enters his territory. The older cat says, "Who let you in? One cat's enough. I don't want to share my stuff." He ends up giving the younger cat advice, and they become friends. Students will enjoy Ehlert's cut paper figures that they can try to emulate. She wrote another charming story called *Feathers for Lunch* in which she identifies the many birds the cat tries to catch with no success.

My Friend Gorilla, written and illustrated by Atsuko Morozumi, is another interesting story about a child and an animal. When the zoo is closed, the zookeeper brings a gorilla home to live for a while. At first his young son is afraid of the huge animal, but soon they become friends. The brief text (a good choice for a slow reader) can be amplified by the student reading aloud by encouraging children to talk about the beautiful detailed illustrations.

Fantasies are also good choices for middle school students to read aloud to young children, especially when they tell about funny children who do crazy things. A good example is *Harold and the Purple Crayon* by Crockett Johnson. Harold literally creates his world with a crayon as the story evolves.

Some stories by Dr. Seuss would be good choices, too, for example, *The 500 Hats of Bartholomew Cubbins, McElligott's Pool*, or *The Cat in the Hat*. Tomi Ungerer's *Moon Man* tells of the man in the moon's trip to earth. Note that these old favorites may be out of print, but you can usually find copies in the public library.

Help slower readers select titles such as *The Littlest Duckling*, written by Gail Herman and illustrated by Ann Schweninger, to read aloud. The repetitious rhythmic language in this book is especially appropriate for small children, and they will enjoy the illustrations. Another humorous book is *Nice Work, Little Wolf!*, written and illustrated by Hilda Offen. A baby wolf scrambles out of his buggy while his mother is inside a store. Over the fence he goes right into the Porkers' cucumber garden! Surprised, the Porker family cannot imagine what he is—a rabbit, a weasel—finally, they decide he's a puppy, so they teach him tricks. Then, they begin to assign him jobs until at last he builds them a swimming pool and a house. By then, he has grown up considerably, and he refuses to work, instead chasing them down the path and far away. Then, he sits down to howl for his mother. She comes running and says, "How you've grown," and admires the house that they can now live in—another role reversal for the wolf that is great fun.

Some realistic stories are engaging and may introduce topics children can talk about. June Jordan, for example, tells about making room for a new baby in *New Life: New Room*. Barbara Williams writes about an up-to-date grandmother in *Kevin's Grandma*. Joan M. Lexau writes charming books such as *I Should Have Stayed in Bed* in which Sam, a young boy, oversleeps, then everything goes wrong. Amy Hest writes about a family's preparation for Grandmother's birthday party in *Nana's Birthday Party*, illustrated by Amy Schwartz. Hest also wrote *The Purple Coat* and *Fancy Aunt Jess*, which has been praised for its "universal quality." Family stories are always appealing.

Increasing Student Involvement With Books

We need to think of different ways of involving students with books if they are going to improve their reading abilities. Try some of the following ideas.

A Reading Marathon

Challenge students to a marathon to see how many different picture books they can read during one month. Establish such rules as these:

1. You must read every page of the book.
2. You must write a one-page summary about the book.

Bring in many picture books so that students will not run out of titles to read, as you begin. The purpose of reading a quantity of books should be made clear, perhaps so that they can select a book or two to record or to share with a second-grade class. Ask the librarian to select a nice variety for you, including some of the following:

The Boy Who Held Back the Sea, retold by Lenny Hort and illustrated by Thomas Locker. This is an old story from the Netherlands with oil paintings not unlike those by noted Dutch artists.

The Giraffe That Walked to Paris, written by Nancy Milton and illustrated by Roger Roth. To settle a disagreement with France the pasha of Egypt gives the king of France a giraffe. After being shipped to France, the giraffe is parked in a town south of Paris until he can be presented to the king. When the presenters can't decide how to get him to Paris, they decide that he can walk!

Visiting the Library

Studies show that only a small percentage of children and young adults go to the library regularly. If we want students to become lifelong readers, we need to encourage them to use their local libraries. Take students to the nearest public library so that they can obtain library cards and explore what a library has to offer. In Thinking + Lesson Plan 4 in Appendix A (see page 145) is a plan you might use for presenting this activity.

Introduce Thinking + Lesson Plan 4 by reading William Miller's picture book *Richard Wright and the Library Card*. This true story of Richard Wright's determination to read is based on a segment of Wright's autobiographical book *Black Boy*. Miller tells the story of Richard's learning to read. However, when he does finally learn to read, he has no money to buy books, and blacks at the time were not permitted to borrow books from the library. A friendly white man lends him his own library card so Richard can check out books to read. Through reading Richard discovers that others like him also struggled for freedom. As he writes, "Every page was a ticket to freedom."

Another picture book that is informative about libraries is Lisl Weil's *Let's Go to the Library*. This book not only describes the different offerings of libraries today but it also tells how libraries began in such places as Alexandria in ancient Egypt.

Talking About the Need for Books

Do we still need books? With the emphasis on computer technology, students might discuss the advantages and disadvantages of what books offer. George

Ella Lyon's book titled *Book* provides an interesting consideration of what books have to offer and suggests avenues for investigation. The author presents exciting metaphors for the book as a house, chest, and farm as she challenges readers to think about what books can mean. Full-page paintings by Peter Catalanotto enhance Lyon's ideas. Students might consider other metaphors for the book, perhaps writing short poems—couplets, cinquains, or haiku—about the book and its place in our lives.

Conclusion

In this chapter we have addressed how teaching with picture books can strengthen the growth of reading abilities. Beginning with a strong emphasis on oral language development as a foundation for reading, I suggested the use of such skills as storytelling and reading aloud to younger children. I also recommended using a listening center for gifted students as well as slower readers who can benefit from the support of recorded stories. In Chapter 4 we will examine additional ways of developing literacy skills with particular attention to writing.

From *When I Was Young in the Mountains* by Cynthia Rylant, illustrated by Diane Goode, copyright ©1982 by Diane Goode, illustrations. Used by permission of Dutton Children's Books, a division of Penguin Putnam Inc.

CHAPTER 4

Stimulating Thinking, Talking, and Writing

Picture books provide varied stimuli that can lead to talking and then writing. You may also feature word play, repetitive or cumulative language patterns, and examples of different literary genres that students can examine and use as models for writing. Students who have difficulty writing and limited-English-proficient or non–English-speaking students especially need the support of model forms and sentence structures.

Focusing on Language

Use picture books to introduce fun with language for students of all ability levels. Word play challenges middle school students to think creatively. It also teaches them to enjoy reading and writing in a way they may not have experienced previously, and it may interest them in other aspects of language, even grammar!

Show students how writers can play with words by reading *Double Trouble in Walla Walla*, written by Andrew Clements and illustrated by Salvatore Murdocca. This author tells a story remarkably full of words that are doublets, rhymes, or just plain repetitions such as *tutu, hip-hop, Henny Penny, Humpty Dumpty, pow-wow, chit-chat, brain-drain*, and so on. Students may have fun suggesting other examples of this type of word that is surprisingly prevalent in English. Create a word wall on which students' words are collected over a month. This list can be on a large chalkboard or a long sheet of butcher paper mounted on the wall. Students then can create short poems using some of the words displayed.

Students will be delighted also to read books by actor Fred Gwynne, whose photograph they may recognize as the star of *The Munsters*. He has written and illustrated several books that focus on funny misinterpretations of homonyms and common idioms as in *A Chocolate Moose for Dinner*. Although his books are old, they are so popular that you probably can find at least one in your local library. Other titles by Gwynne include *The King Who Rained* and *The Sixteen Hand Horse*. Students can write and illustrate examples of these hilarious plays on words. Such activities make them aware of confusing spellings as they sort out which spelling goes with which meaning—*bear, bare* or *pear, pair, pare*—and talk about the odd expressions we often use, as in "holding up a bank."

As mentioned in the previous chapter, Peggy Parish's Amelia Bedelia books consist of a whole series of books that are now being continued by her nephew. One humorous title in the series is *Thank You, Amelia Bedelia*. Amelia Bedelia is a maid who has trouble following directions because she applies a literal meaning to the words she hears. If, for example, you told Amelia to "butter up" her boss, she would spread butter on him or her from head to toe. Students can brainstorm examples of other actions that are quite humorous if taken literally. Let them illustrate a situation, printing one or two sentences below revealing what Amelia was supposed to do.

Ounce Dice Trice, written by Alastair Reid and illustrated by Ben Shahn, is an old book, but well worth searching for in used book shops. Gifted students will love creating garlands of words like those Reid includes in this book, beginning, for example, with "What is a *hamburgler*?"

Loud Emily, written by Alexis O'Neill and illustrated by Nancy Carpenter, tells of a girl whose voice was so loud that she had to enroll in a school to teach her to be soft spoken. However, Emily finds a good use for her loud voice that saves a sailing ship lost in the fog. Students might create a word wall of Talking Words, discussing their meanings from *whisper* to *shriek*.

Once students become involved with language, they may be interested in other kinds of information about language that ties more closely to the writing process. For example, Ruth Heller has written and illustrated several attractive picture books on the parts of speech. Her first book was *Merry-Go-Round: A Book About Nouns*. Her colorful illustrations enhance the informative text. Another title is *Mine, All Mine: A Book About Pronouns*. Imagine a book that makes using pronouns fun! The bold colors and the humor of the illustrations add interest to what can be a dull subject. Heller also wrote *A Cache of Jewels and Other Collective Nouns; Kites*

Sail High: A Book About Verbs; Many Luscious Lollipops: A Book About Adjectives; Up, Up and Away: A Book About Adverbs; and *Behind the Mask: A Book About Prepositions.*

Other books to look for that focus on language include the following:

Fingers Are Always Bringing Me News by Mary O'Neill. This book is about words related to movements of fingers—tapping, grabbing, and so on.

What Is That Sound? by Mary O'Neill. O'Neill writes about words that label sounds in this book.

Crash, Bang, Boom by Peter Spier. Spier focuses on onomatopoeia, words that sound like what they mean.

Patterns That Invite Students to Write

A number of picture books present interesting, sometimes humorous, patterns that students enjoy imitating. Because the patterns are simple to follow, most students will have a successful writing experience. Although these patterns are especially helpful for less able students, talented middle schoolers will find them challenging and enjoyable, too.

Bill Martin Jr's pattern book *Brown Bear, Brown Bear, What Do You See?* is a great book for developing beginning literacy skills. Illustrated with large colorful figures by Eric Carle, it sets up a pattern that students quickly grasp, joining in with the reader as each page is turned. The brown bear sees "a redbird looking at me," so of course, the next page is filled with a large redbird. After reading this book several times, the group can chant the full text, and can recognize the pattern used by the author. Working in small groups, students can create a similar book, perhaps beginning with "Black cat, black cat, what do you see? I see a white horse wearing a hat!" Students can present this lesson to younger students, engaging children in composing a book, too.

Barn Cat, written by Carol P. Saul and illustrated by Mary Azarian, is a counting book that begins information about each number with these words: "Barn cat at the red door,/Barncat, what are you looking for?" Rhyming couplets provide an answer. The illustrations in this picture book are exceptionally distinctive. Students could choose another animal, making their own opening line, for example, "Hello, Mr. Brown Bear,/ Why are you going to the fair?"

A.H. Benjamin's book *It Could Have Been Worse*, illustrated by Tim Warnes, is a story of a mouse's adventures that uses words and illustrations to present a threatening situation and the fortuitous result. For example, the mouse falls into a dark hole, but by doing so, as shown only in the illustrations, he escapes being caught by a raptor. After each escape, the narrator inserts, "It could have been worse!"

Alexander and His Terrible, Horrible, No Good, Very Bad Day by Judith Viorst is a funny story that students will enjoy and identify with. A kind of listing narrative, it defines structured information that students can report. After reading this story aloud, ask students to list all the bad things that happened to Alexander. Write this list on the board, then have students write a summary paragraph telling about things that happened to Alexander to make him conclude that this was not one of his best days.

What do you think about when you can't get to sleep? Marc Sutherland explores this topic in *The Waiting Place*. He writes engaging quatrains about the ideas that flit through a young boy's mind as he lies in bed waiting to fall asleep. Sutherland also has created intriguing black and white full-page illustrations to accompany his poems. Students can discuss this topic in cooperative groups, then each group can create a poem and illustration to share with the class or with younger students. Selected gifted students could plan to teach this writing lesson to a group of third or fourth graders following the methods you used in presenting it to them.

Other books that present similar patterns for writing include the following:

Everybody Needs a Rock, written by Byrd Baylor and illustrated by Peter Parnall (Also see *The Desert Is Theirs* and *I'm in Charge of Celebrations*)

Fortunately by Remy Charlip

Wow! It's Great Being a Duck by Joan Rankin

Happiness Is a Warm Puppy by Charles Schulz

Composing Poetry

Many students enjoy writing poetry. Given sufficient guidance, most of them can create surprisingly satisfying poems. The picture books described in the following sections suggest stimuli you might find helpful in teaching students to write poetry.

Short Poems About Common Objects

When students are introduced to free verse, many of them realize that poetry writing is not an impossible task for them. Students might work in pairs to create poems after reading a few by John Updike published in *A Helpful Alphabet of Friendly Objects*. Present several of Updike's poems on transparencies.

Charlotte Zolotow wrote pleasant verses about nature in *All That Sunlight* illustrated by Walter Stein. The simple patterns used are varied, but they are forms that most students could imitate successfully, for example:

Sing, sing, sing
Crickets sing
Birds sing
Kettles sing
Radiators sing
Violins sing
Leaves in trees sing
And sometimes mothers sing
Sing sing sing.

Other collections of poetry that may inspire students to write poetry include Jack Prelutsky's comical poems, which are popular with middle school students. He has written many books of poetry, but one you might especially enjoy is *The Gargoyle on the Roof*, illustrated by Peter Sís. These poems have intriguing titles such as "Lament of a Lonely Troll," "Bugaboo," "My Sister Is a Werewolf," and "Plaint of the Headless Horseman." Students might work in pairs or small groups to compose funny poems like those Prelutsky wrote.

Another collection of humorous verses is *The Bookworm's Feast: A Potluck of Poems*, written by J. Patrick Lewis and illustrated by John O'Brien. This poet has fun with language, using alliteration, puns, and so on.

Poetry Focused on a Theme

Read a few of the funny poems collected by Nadine Bernard Westcott in *Never Take a Pig to Lunch and Other Poems About the Fun of Eating*. Her illustrations may inspire students to create humorous art to accompany their own original verses. Poems include those by contemporary poets and old favorites that may be new to children, such as this one:

I eat my peas with honey;
I've done it all my life.
It makes the peas taste funny,
But it keeps them on the knife.

In contrast to Westcott's collection is *Cats Are Cats*, compiled by Nancy Larrick and illustrated by Ed Young. Cat lovers will enjoy the pictures created by both words and art. Some poems like Vachel Lindsay's "I Saw a Proud, Mysterious Cat" are wonderful for choric speaking. Point out the varied forms used by these poets as you invite students to create original work.

Another book that focuses on cats is *Cat Up a Tree*, written by Anne Isaacs and illustrated by Stephen Mackey. The poet uses a variety of poetic forms that may interest your students. For example, one poem is a conversation comprising couplets spoken by a girl and her father. Another is composed of rhymed lists. Students who try these forms can decide whether they want to use rhyme as free verse works just as well. Share these books and others focused on different topics so students have choices about subjects.

Kristine O'Connell George offers different perspectives of trees in *Old Elm Speaks: Tree Poems*, illustrated with lovely oils by Kate Kiesler. Writing poems about trees ties in well with science studies as students learn to identify local trees and take time to admire the bark and the structure of each tree.

Mary O'Neill focuses on colors in *Hailstones and Halibut Bones: Adventures in Color*. This book was presented as a film by Weston Woods. Almost all students create impressive verses as they enumerate the many things associated with each color. O'Neill uses rhyme, but free verse is just as effective.

Japanese Haiku

Show students several examples of traditional haiku. Have them identify the general characteristics of this short form of poetry: (a) The poet talks about nature, (b) There are usually three lines, and (c) Each poem contains 17 syllables. Then, students can try writing original poems, a fitting culminating activity for a study of Japan. The following picture books provide examples:

My Own Rhythm: An Approach to Haiku by Ann Atwood tells the stories of three masters of Japanese haiku—Basho, Issa, and Buson—giving examples of each. The book is illustrated beautifully. Atwood developed a second book of her own poems, *Haiku: Vision in Poetry and Photography*.

In *Cricket Songs*, Harry Behn translated the original Japanese haiku. The poems are presented with art by Japanese masters in an attractive small volume.

In a Spring Garden, a collection by Richard Lewis that is illustrated handsomely by Ezra Jack Keats, is one of the best poetry volumes for young people.

Exploring Short Prose Forms

In addition to poetry, in this section I focus on short forms of prose that may seem more approachable and enjoyable for students who are just learning to control writing as a means of expression. Diaries, letters, and folklore such as the pourquoi tale offer interesting possibilities for engaging students in writing across the curriculum. For each form discussed there are intriguing picture books to use as models for writing.

Using Story Starters

Use alphabet books to suggest Story Starter material (prompts), for example, Norma Farber's *I Found Them in the Yellow Pages*. Duplicate selected pages from these books to give to pairs of students who work together to compose a story based on what appears on that page. Other alphabet books are listed in Chapter 8.

Chris Van Allsburg's *The Mysteries of Harris Burdick* is a wonderful collection of pictures that you can put to instant use for motivating student writing. Each full-page picture bears a provocative caption plus an interesting line that will stimulate students' thinking. Photocopy a few of these pictures for classroom use, giving one to each small group. Students can brainstorm ideas about what the picture suggests and then compose a narrative together.

Writing Diaries or Journals

The diary or journal is a form that recently has become more popular in adult and children's literature. As students try writing this form, however, they should write something more imaginative than just the facts: "I got up at 7:00 and ate my breakfast. I arrived at school at 8:25. I went to English and science, then to lunch at 11:45…." Either of the following books will suggest different approaches to writing diaries that another person might enjoy reading.

Diary of a Drummer Boy, written by Marlene Targ Brill and illustrated by Michael Garland, is a fictional journal based on historical research, telling something about the lives of a real boy and his brother who were drummers during the U.S. Civil War. The author writes in the preface: "This book is what I imagine Orion might have written had he kept a journal." Full-page paintings enhance the text, and an afterword tells the reader what happened to the real Orion after the war. Here is an excellent stimulus for gifted students who can combine their knowledge of history with language arts skills to produce an imaginative recounting of real events.

Marissa Moss's *Amelia Takes Command* is a wonderfully imaginative book that can be used when students are beginning to write journals or logs. It provides a clear idea of the kinds of pictures and drawings that can be integrated into a record of information. You might put several of the pages on transparencies to share with the students. Amelia is a fifth-grade girl who records the troubles she has over the school year and how she solves her problems.

Writing Letters

Many people do not like to write letters, yet they are an important part of our lives. Picture books may help you engage students in enjoyable experiences with varied kinds of letters.

Janet and Allan Ahlberg's *The Jolly Postman or Other People's Letters* is a humorous book with real letters inside, suggesting all kinds of letter writing. Examples are provided for postcards, invitations, thank-you notes, and so forth. This book also provides an interesting model for creating a book for children.

In Schim Schimmel's *Dear Children of the Earth: A Letter From Home*, Mother Earth writes a letter to young people about caring for the planet and all the animals that inhabit it. Acrylic paintings by the author/illustrator make this a very attractive resource. Students can write shorter letters about something they care about, perhaps pretending to be a tool or an object in their living rooms that speaks to the people who use it. Or, they might write a response to Mother Earth.

Another humorous approach to letter writing is *Dear Dragon...and Other Useful Letter Forms for Young Ladies and Gentlemen Engaged in Everyday Correspondence*, written by Sesyle Joslin and illustrated by Irene Haas. Each letter form is introduced and written quite seriously and in good form. However, the illustrations add hilarious situations. For example, when you are traveling up the Amazon River and a friendly native queen insists on having you for dinner, you write the usual letter to a friend, ending, "Wish you were here." The illustration shows *you* writing the letter while seated in a large pot over a fire being prepared for a cannibal's dinner.

Helping Students Write Stories

Short narrative forms of writing—jokes, fables, and tall tales—are useful for young writers to attempt as they gain confidence in their writing ability. Thinking + Lesson Plan 5 in Appendix A (see page 146) shows students how to write the pourquoi tale, a story that explains *why* a natural phenomenon occurs, for example, why the sun rises in the east and sets in the west. *Pourquoi* means *why* in French. Many examples of these stories can be found in Native American lore as well as in the literature of other countries.

Other books that you might use as models for pourquoi tales are as follows:

The Story of Lightning & Thunder by Ashley Bryan. This book explains how two sheep, Thunder and Lightning, moved from West Africa to the sky.

How the Rooster Got His Crown by Amy Lowry Poole. Based on a Chinese tale with art by the author, this work may inspire students to create a book.

Writing Nonfiction

Sometimes we emphasize the writing of stories and we forget to teach students how to write expository forms. Here are suggestions for engaging students with writing nonfiction.

Writing Biographies

Writing short biographies of famous historical figures provides an excellent culminating activity for the study of a specific time period. This project is especially appropriate in a social studies class as students study the contributions of people of different races and ethnic groups to the development of the United States. Contributions to various subject areas can be featured, as appropriate.

Numerous picture book biographies can serve as models that students can imitate for a rewarding writing experience. Have students observe different approaches to writing based on a person's life—autobiography, stories that have an autobiographical base, factual biography, and biographical narrative. Approaches to autobiography are featured in the first theme in Chapter 9. In this chapter I focus on two ways of handling biography, that is, works written by one person about another person's life. Following are two authors whose work fits each category. Many other biographies are discussed in Chapter 7.

David A. Adler wrote *A Picture Book of Sojourner Truth*, illustrated by Gershom Griffith. You will find many additional titles by Adler featuring such famous U.S. historical figures as Martin Luther King, Helen Keller, Jesse Owens, Eleanor Roosevelt, Sitting Bull, and Frederick Douglass. Although Adler uses some narrative features, his work follows a rather traditional factual biographical format.

Faith Ringgold's *My Dream of Martin Luther King* is an unusual biography that begins with the author's dream of young Martin and the events that led up to his delivering the "I Have a Dream" speech. Ringgold is known for her story quilts. In this book she uses the same folk-modern style of art to tell Martin Luther King's story. Ringgold's story is based on facts about King's life, but it has a strong narrative tone including an element of fantasy. Ringgold wrote another biography with this same kind of fantasy about Sojourner Truth (see Chapter 8 where I discuss Ringgold's art).

Expository Writing

Students should learn to research a topic that especially interests them. They can plan to write an I-Search paper, as described by Ken Macrorie in *Searching Writing* (1994). If two or more students want to work together, this can become a We-Search paper. The main thing is that they use a variety of resources, such as interviews, the telephone book, telephone calls, letters, the Internet, and so on.

For example, students who want to find out how to select a good horse for purchase might begin with an overview about horses. A beautiful oversized picture book, *Horses: History, Behavior, Breeds, Riding, Jumping,* written by Jackie Budd, presents a wealth of information that provides an excellent overview. A variety of illustrations from small drawings in the margins showing the grooming process to a double-page fold-out showing the details of a large stable complements the text. Students will be impressed by the large painting of wild horses running down a stream and the picture of the horses racing down a track. A world map locates the many members of the *equus* (equine) group, and a table identifies the more than 200 breeds of horses and ponies. After perusing this informative book, students should search at least three other sources, as mentioned.

A student who has heard about problems people are having with lice might like to investigate that topic. A well-done picture book such as *Yikes-Lice!* by Donna Caffey with illustrations by Patrick Girouard would be a good place to begin the research. Then, the student could interview the school nurse or a doctor, talk to a science teacher, or visit sites on the Internet to get different viewpoints and information.

A pair of students who are particularly interested in art and have heard about Monet or seen his work might investigate his life. In this case an intriguing picture book to suggest is *Linnea in Monet's Garden,* written by Christina Bjork and illustrated by Lena Anderson. This is a more interesting approach than beginning with the encyclopedia, as students may be accustomed to doing.

Writing an Interview

Students can write interview schedules, that is, the questions they plan to ask at an actual interview. Such schedules could be prepared before an author visits the school or a local bookstore. Schedules also could be mailed to authors who may answer at least some of the questions.

Another interesting variation is to plan an interview of a fictional character, for example, Cinderella or the wicked stepmother. Two students could work together with one being the interviewer and the other the interviewee. A pair of students could plan a very humorous interview to be performed before the class. Just think of the possibilities if one student were to interview Amelia Bedelia.

Writing How–To Books

Encourage students to write about something they know how to do. Picture books offer models for writing how-to books, although they are much longer than students' writing probably will be. A book that will interest some girls and boys is The _Most Excellent_ Book of How to Be a Cheerleader, written by Bob Kiralfy and illustrated by Rob Shone and Peter Harper. Although this book is only 32 pages long, it is full of information including sample cheers and chants, directions for making uniforms and pom-poms, and many performance tips.

Writing a Newspaper

Composing a newspaper is a real challenge for a class. They will need to study different newspapers to identify all the kinds of writing and art that appear in this type of publication. Picture books may suggest various approaches to newspaper writing. One idea is The Stone Age News, written by Fiona MacDonald and illustrated by a team from Walker Books. Of course, a newspaper in the Stone Age has to be fictional; yet the information presented is based on history. Much humor is included, too, such as in the advertising. This is a great writing-across-the-curriculum strategy.

Getting to Know Writers and How They Work

It is important to tell students about authors whose work we are reading. As mentioned in Chapter 8, we also need to introduce the artists who illustrate these wonderful picture books.

Introducing an Author to the Class

Have authors or illustrators come to your school as often as possible, or arrange to take your students to a presentation scheduled at a nearby library or bookstore. Marc Brown, who wrote and illustrated a number of picture books about an aardvark named Arthur, told a class he was visiting in a local school that one of his teachers told him, "If you want to be successful, do what you love doing and do it as well as you can," and he added, "That was the best advice I ever got."

When I was asked to introduce Paul Zindel as a speaker at a teachers' workshop, I began by reading his lovely picture book *I Love My Mother*, illustrated by John Melo. Most of the teachers in the audience did not know this autobiographical book, which provides insight into the background of an interesting man who is much better known for such young adult novels as *The Pigman* and *Reef of Death*.

You might introduce an author whose work you are going to study by first reading aloud a picture book by that author. Many authors who are well known for writing different genres later discover the picture book as an appealing way to share their thinking. Well-known novelist Toni Morrison, for example, wrote *The Big Box* with her son Slade Morrison; the book is illustrated by Giselle Potter. Noted poet Lucille Clifton wrote picture books about an African American boy. One title is *Some of the Days of Everett Anderson*, illustrated by Evaline Ness, which contains the line, "Being six/is full of tricks/and Everett Anderson knows it." She also wrote *Good Times*, which deals with the death of a father, and *The Times They Used to Be*, illustrated by Susan Jeschke. These books all feature a positive view of family life.

Studying the Work of One Writer

The project described in the Thinking + Project on the next page focuses on the work of one writer, beginning with a picture book, then reading an age-appropriate novel and extending to the whole body of this author's work. In this case the author selected is Cynthia Rylant who has written novels for adolescents as well as picture books. She has authored autobiographical material and has even illustrated some of her own work. This is a good activity for the first weeks of school.

The Thinking + Project will last at least a month because the novel suggested contains 12 short chapters and time is required for the other activities. You need to allow for discussion and journal writing related to *Missing May* because this novel presents several themes that you will want to develop.

Thinking + Project
Title of Project: Getting to Know an Author

Expected Outcomes

The learner will

1. read a number of books by one author.
2. search for information about this author.
3. write a short essay about the work of the author.

Teaching/Learning Strategy

Resources: Focus on Cynthia Rylant. Locate books written by Rylant and books about her and her writing. Locate at least one copy of *Missing May*, which won the Newbery Award, to read aloud, and a copy of *When I Was Young in the Mountains*.

Directions

Before beginning the novel, read aloud Rylant's autobiographical picture book *When I Was Young in the Mountains* as a way of introducing Cynthia Rylant. Then, begin reading *Missing May* a chapter at a time.

Step I: Divide the class into cooperative learning groups (CLGs) to focus on aspects of this study of an author's life and work. Assign each group a specific task to accomplish while you are reading the novel, for example:

    CLG 1: Read two picture books by Rylant. Evaluate the content and illustration, and compare the two books.

    CLG 2: Research the Internet to gather information about this author; plan a way to present findings to the class.

    CLG 3: Read *Best Wishes*, then summarize findings about Rylant's life.

    CLG 4: Make a list of all books by Rylant, including publishing data.

    CLG 5: Write a letter to Cynthia Rylant requesting information about her recommendations for young writers.

Step II: Have each group report its work to the class and display its findings on a large corkboard labeled with the author's name.

Step III: Have one person from each CLG form a committee to plan a collage on a large sheet of paper about Rylant's life and work. Members of the CLGs will contribute various artwork to the class project.

Assessment Performance

1. Each student will keep a process journal in which to record responses to the book being read aloud and to the CLG project.
2. Each student will write a three to five paragraph essay about Rylant and her work.

Notice that I selected a highly respected author to study and chose to introduce students to her by reading aloud one of her best-known books, *When I Was Young in the Mountains*, to the class. (See the illustration on page 46.) You might use one of Rylant's newer picture books, *Tulip Sees America*, which tells how she moved west from Ohio to Oregon. This autobiographical picture book also conveys the message that every U.S. state has something wonderful to appreciate.

Here is a sampling of picture books by Cynthia Rylant:

An Angel for Solomon, illustrated by Peter Catalanotto.

Appalachia: The Voices of Sleeping Birds, illustrated by Barry Moser. This nonfiction book is a sensitive picture of Appalachian people and their lives.

Margaret, Frank, and Andy: Three Writers' Stories. This book contains brief biographies of Margaret Wise Brown, L. Frank Baum, and E.B. White.

Poppleton Forever, illustrated by Mark Teague. This is the fourth book Rylant wrote about Poppleton.

Tulip Sees America, illustrated by Lisa Desimini.

When I Was Young in the Mountains, illustrated by Diane Goode. This outstanding Caldecott Honor Book is autobiographical, telling of a child living with grandparents in West Virginia's coal-mining region.

Before presenting this author study project, you will need to read the novel well in advance in order to deal with the themes of death and grief presented and to take full advantage of learning activities the book suggests.

Rylant's novel *Missing May* won the Newbery Award, the award given annually by the American Library Association for the best book written for young people. This award is named for an early publisher of children's books. Your librarian can probably provide a list of other books, usually short novels, that have won this award, if you are interested. As mentioned in Chapter 1, the Caldecott Award is given annually for the best illustrations in a children's book (see Appendix B for a complete list of winners.)

The kind of study presented in the Thinking + Project could be adapted in various ways. Each cooperative learning group, for example, might later focus on another author who would then be introduced to the class. If that activity followed a class study of one author's work, as presented here, students would already be familiar with the process.

Keeping a log or process journal throughout this focused study helps students be aware of what they are learning. Group sharing of individual journal responses periodically is important for all students. Hearing what others have written suggests different ideas that students might apply in their next project.

Other Authors Recommended for Study

A number of other authors have written both picture books as well as young adult or adult books. Their work might be featured in a study similar to that described in the Thinking + Project. The following authors are recommended: Rudolfo Anaya, Natalie Babbitt, Jean Fritz, Robert McCloskey, Amy Tan, and Jane Yolen.

Conclusion

In this chapter we have looked at picture books as a means of stimulating thinking, talking, and writing. First, I recommended picture books that provide humorous approaches to language study and books that suggest interesting patterns that students can imitate. Realizing that many middle school students need considerable assistance with writing, I then discussed short forms of both fiction and nonfiction that students might compose successfully. I concluded this chapter with a sample study of the work of one author who has written both picture books and books for young adults. In Chapter 5 we will explore more ways of extending students' knowledge about language and literature.

HAPPY BIRTHDAY

Feliz Cumpleaños

Bonne Anniversaire

Χρονια Πολλα

Buon Compleanno

𝕲𝖊𝖇𝖚𝖗𝖙𝖘𝖙𝖆𝖌𝖘𝖜𝖚̈𝖓𝖘𝖈𝖍𝖊

STO LAT!

祝
生
日
快
樂

CHAPTER 5

Extending Student Knowledge About Language and Literature

Few middle school students have really studied language or literature. They have much to learn, therefore, about English and other languages around the world. They also need to learn more about the various genres and components of narrative: plot, characterization, setting, theme, and so forth. They can benefit from instruction that focuses on literary devices such as imagery, point of view, and elements of style. Picture books often can assist you in planning lessons around these devices.

Learning About Language

Many aspects of language could be introduced to middle school students through the use of exemplary picture books, for example, writing in ancient times, the history of English, or information about the many languages spoken in other countries. Here is a sampling of the kinds of language topics presented in picture book format.

Scrawl! Writing in Ancient Times is a fascinating nonfiction book about the beginnings of writing. Prepared by the Geography Department of Runestone Press, it presents information about early writing systems in the Middle East and Mediterranean regions as well as in China and the Americas. This overview of early writing could provide the basis for further research by groups of students.

The history of the English language is another intriguing topic of study. Donna Brook wrote and Jean Day Zallinger illustrated a fine summary of this topic titled *The Journey of English*. The author first presents English as a worldwide language of commerce and then introduces its Indo-European roots. Thus, students learn much about European history and then American history as English spread to North America. The author ends with a brief introduction to the study of regional dialects in the United States and includes some information about word origins in the Appendix. Additional books of interest to students and resources for teachers are listed.

Dialectology is also present in picture books that tell stories featuring different cultures and regions of the United States. For example, Gloria Jean Pinkney and artist Jerry Pinkney describe the trip from a northern city that a young African American girl makes to North Carolina to visit family. Titled *Back Home*, this story includes dialogue that seems to model authentic rural African American speech. For example, when Uncle June meets Ernestine at the train, he says warmly, "Hey, Ernestine! I knew right off it was you. I do declare, if you don't favor my oldest sister Zulah when she was a girl." Students might consider which elements of such dialogue are phrases that they might commonly use themselves, and which ones are different. If they would never say, for example, "I do declare," what might they say instead? Be careful to emphasize that various dialects are different, but not wrong. We all can share interesting expressions that we learned within our families. The speech sample from *Back Home* also suggests an intriguing study of names and naming practices.

Eve Merriam wrote a book that focuses on names for groups of things in *A Gaggle of Geese*. After reading this book, students could generate a list on a word wall, including *herd, school, pride, covey, gang, team*, and so on. Judith Rossner wrote a book that features homonyms, titled *What Kind of Feet Does a Bear Have?*. A list of homonyms could be added to a word wall, along with other categories of words you choose to introduce—acronyms, pseudonyms, or synonyms. Students could create a mini-thesaurus with these words designed to assist them when they write.

Students also might learn to use sign language by studying picture books that present sign. One example is *Handtalk: An ABC of Finger Spelling & Sign Language*, written by Remy Charlip and Mary Beth and illustrated with photographs by George Ancona. As the authors suggest, if students want to know more they should interview a deaf person.

An introduction to the Chinese language is provided by Peggy Goldstein in *Long Is a Dragon: Chinese Writing for Children*. Although Goldstein did the calligraphy throughout, the cover art and design are done by Jos Sances. Goldstein explains how ideographic writing evolved from tracks in the earth to symbols to modern-day characters that are further removed from real objects. She teaches basic vocabulary and explains briefly how other Asian writing developed from the Chinese. Students might enjoy trying the artful calligraphy to produce good wishes typical of the Chinese New Year banners shown in this book. This introduction might lead to inviting immigrant parents or grandparents to the classroom to share their native languages.

Also, share with students books written in other languages, for example, *Los Gnomos* by Dutch writer Wil Huygen and illustrator Rien Poortliet. This book contains charming pop-up scenes that feature the gnomes engaged in various activities; one scene focusing on *los juegos* (games) shows gnomes jumping rope, swinging, and playing other games. Bring in books, too, that include stories or poems in English and another language, for example, versions of *Mulan* or Alma Flor Ada's poetry in *Gathering the Sun: An Alphabet in Spanish and English*, illustrated by Simon Silva. Naomi Nye also has collected poems in Spanish with translations into English in *The Tree Is Older Than You Are: A Bilingual Gathering of Poems and Stories From Mexico*. Students could practice speaking these poems for the PTA. One group can recite the Spanish poem followed by a second group giving the English translation.

Draw students' attention to the different ways of saying and writing "Happy Birthday" (see page 62).

Reading Poetry

Middle school students need to become acquainted with some of the fine poetry that is available to them. The trick is to entice them to read poetry enough so that they come to enjoy it. Picture books may help you in this effort. In addition to the volumes listed elsewhere in this text, examine the following attractive books.

A beautiful collection of poems selected and introduced by Kenneth Koch and Kate Farrell is *Talking to the Sun: An Illustrated Anthology of Poems for Young People*. The illustrations are works of art that have some relation to the poetry presented. As Koch writes, "Our aim was a book that would show how great and how likable poetry is and what a variety of it there is to read." Poems and art selected represent different times and places, so there is something for every purpose.

I'm Nobody! Who Are You?: Poems of Emily Dickinson for Young People, illustrated by Rex Schneider, is an appealing volume. Each poem is framed by a painting that helps explicate the meaning of Dickinson's words. An introduction by Richard B. Sewall supplies pertinent biographical information and anecdotes that students should enjoy. (See the Thinking + Lesson 6 in Appendix A [see page 147].)

A remarkable collection of modern poetry, *Brown Honey in Broomwheat Tea*, focuses on the life of a young African American girl. Written by Joyce Carol Thomas and illustrated by Floyd Cooper, it portrays family life in a positive, loving manner. These poems speak to the middle school age child in a meaningful way.

The Trees Stand Shining: Poetry of the North American Indians includes poetry selected by Hettie Jones with paintings by Robert Andrew Parker. This combination of poetry and art would be a fine volume to use in a study of Native American tribes today and yesterday.

The poetry of Langston Hughes is presented in an attractive volume titled *The Dream Keeper and Other Poems*, illustrated by Brian Pinkney. Middle school students respond positively to these charming poems that deal with familiar subjects. Teachers have often used "Hold Fast to Dreams" to inspire student writing and "Mother to Sun" to point out a fine example of metaphor: life as a stairway. Pinkney's black and white scratchboard illustrations supply a sample of yet another art form students might try.

Celebrating America: A Collection of Poems and Images of the American Spirit is an oversized volume of poems compiled by Laura Whipple with art provided by The Art Institute of Chicago. The poems support many curricular emphases—art, writing, history, and literature. "Smoke Animals" by Rowena Bastin Bennett, one poem in this collection, has been reproduced later in this chapter as an example of extended metaphor to share with students. Many of the short poems included in this collection could be reproduced for classroom displays. This book also offers an interesting introduction to art that could be used before a field trip to an art museum. (Remember, too, that the collections of major museums are available through the Internet.)

After you share picture books of poetry with the class, students can make illustrated poetry posters that present a favorite poem to display on the classroom wall or in the hall where other students can read them. Each student also can select a poem to add to a class collection of poetry titled "Poems We Like."

Exploring Other Genres

As explained in Chapter 4, students need to know more about the various literary genres. They also can experiment with producing some of them. In this chapter I extend the exploration of genres that you can introduce to your students.

Introducing the Fable

The fable is a short narrative that students can compose. Read several by Aesop and other authors. Then, give groups of students a book or two to examine, for example, Marcia Brown's *Once a Mouse...A Fable Cut in Wood*. This tale from India won the Caldecott Award for Brown's woodcuts, another kind of art to share with students. This story will challenge students' thinking as they encounter symbolism and foreshadowing and observe the skillful interweaving of text and illustration.

In addition, middle school students will enjoy the strange and funny fables in *Squids Will Be Squids*, written by Jon Scieszka, illustrated by Lane Smith, and designed by Molly Leach.

Other fables you might use include the following:

Chanticleer and the Fox by Barbara Cooney, which is based on a tale from Chaucer.

Miss Rumphius by Barbara Cooney. This book focuses on creating something beautiful.

Jataka Tales by Nancy DeRoin, which contains fables from India.

Students usually enjoy fables. They can be acted out or read aloud to younger children. Students also can compare different versions of the same story, for example, "The Ant and the Grasshopper." Here is one version that appears in *The Fables of Aesop* as retold by Joseph Jacobs:

> In a field one summer's day a grasshopper was hopping about, chirping and singing to its heart's content. An ant passed by, bearing along with great toil an ear of corn he was taking to the nest.
>
> "Why not come and chat with me," said the grasshopper, "instead of toiling and moiling in that way?"
>
> "I am helping to lay up food for the winter," said the ant, "and I recommend that you do the same."
>
> "Why bother about winter?" said the grasshopper. "We have plenty of food at present."
>
> But the ant went on its way and continued its toil. When the winter came, the grasshopper had no food, and found itself dying of hunger, while it saw the ants distributing every day corn and grain from the stores they had collected in the summer. Then the grasshopper knew—*It is best to prepare for the days of necessity*.

Challenge students to locate other versions of this familiar fable to share with the class.

Thinking + Lesson Plan 7 in Appendix A (see page 148) introduces students to the fable and guides them to produce this genre in cooperative learning groups.

Having Fun With Parody

After reading at least one example of the traditional Cinderella story (see Chapter 7), bring in examples of picture books by authors who use the Cinderella theme in an unusual way to create a parody. For example, Frances Minters interprets the theme for modern times in *Cinder-Elly*. Illustrated by Brian Karas, this humorous tale features the prince as a basketball player and the traditional slipper as a sneaker, which sisters Sue and Nelly try in vain to put on. Another parody is *Slender Ella and Her Fairy Hogfather*, written by Vivian Sathre and illustrated by Sally Anne Lambert, which presents pigs as the characters.

In *Cinder Edna*, Ellen Jackson tells the story of Cinderella's neighbor, Edna, who knew how to "make tuna casserole 16 different ways" and how to "get spots off everything from rugs to ladybugs." Illustrated by Kevin O'Malley, this funny story compares the passive Cinderella with Edna who is strong and spunky and likes to tell jokes. Edna does not believe in fairy godmothers but earns her own way, putting a lovely dress on layaway to wear to the prince's ball. There, she finds the prince to be boring, but falls for his brother, Rupert, who is into recycling and likes to tell jokes, too. The two friends, thereafter known as Ella and Edna, having dropped the Cinder prefix, are married in a double wedding ceremony.

Another version of the Cinderella tale is *Bigfoot Cinderrrrrella*, written by Tony Johnston and illustrated by James Warhola. The Bigfoot family live in the old-growth forest. The Bigfoot prince is "as odoriferous as his tree-home was coniferous"...and so the humor goes. Middle school students will probably love the irreverent language in this book, although some teachers may not!

After sharing parodies of the Cinderella story with students, challenge them to create their own parody based on Cinderella.

Another author who has delighted in creating parodies is Jon Scieszka. For example, he plays with the story of "The Three Little Pigs" in *The True Story of The 3 Little Pigs by A. Wolf*, as told to Jon Scieszka and illustrated by Lane Smith. Other similar parodies based on this same story are described in the section "Exploring Stereotyped Thinking" in Chapter 6.

An older book that suggests delightful parodies that students could try to imitate in their writing is Eve Merriam's *The Inner City Mother Goose*, illustrated by Lawrence Ratzkin. This book is worth looking for in local libraries or a used bookstore. One example from this collection of poetry is the parody of "Pussy Cat, Pussy Cat" which contains an example of irony. The cat says it has gone to a hearing at City Hall, but couldn't get in. Why? Although the hearing was about cats and their habitats, "they only admitted dogs and rats."

Discovering Imagery

One of the best sources of examples of imagery, as mentioned earlier, is poetry. However, many fine examples also may be found in picture books.

Similes and Metaphors

A wonderful picture book that contains outstanding examples of imagery is *Sound of Sunshine, Sound of Rain*, written by Florence Heide and illustrated by Kenneth Longtemps. Read the story aloud and then ask students to talk about the language used by the author. They will probably remember such similes as "his voice is like a kitten curled on my shoulder." This book has much more to offer in terms of plot and characterization, as will be discussed later.

Author Peter Nickl plays with trite similes, for example, "as fierce as a wolf" and "as wise as an owl," in *The Story of the Kind Wolf*, illustrated by Josef Wilkon and translated from the German by Marion Koenig. Nickl has concocted a humorous story about a wolf who "starts a new way of life" and becomes a doctor. He saves a half-frozen little rabbit, and he puts a sick fox on a vegetarian diet. The owl keeps saying, "Once a wolf, always a wolf," but no one listens to him. Students might have fun listing all the familiar similes we have used so much that they have become clichés: "busy as a bee," "clever as a fox," "quiet as a mouse," and so on. Then, they can try to create more interesting comparisons, for example, "as quiet as a feather falling on the snow." They can use these images in original poems.

Personification

You also will find examples of personification in both poetry and prose. G. Brian Karas uses personification in *The Windy Day*. He tells of a little breeze that "peeled off the trade winds" and went off on its own to stir up mischief in a tidy town. It skipped and whistled over the choppy seas and swept up papers and pancakes and photographs in Bernard's town.

A picture book that personifies a tree is Holling Clancy Holling's *Tree in the Trail*. This book is by a fine artist and writer who is known for such titles as *Pagoo* and *Minn of the Mississippi*, the tale about a little canoe that travels down the mighty Mississippi River. In *Tree in the Trail* the main character is a tree that grew along the Santa Fe Trail. The story begins with a young Indian boy's recognition of the cottonwood sapling:

"Ho! Young tree," he cried, "for days I have seen none of your tribe. How did you come to be the only tree on this empty plain?" Just then a breeze swept up the slope and rustled the sapling's leaves.

"I Like to See It Lap the Miles"

I like to see it lap the miles,
And lick the valleys up,
And stop to feed itself at tanks,
And then, prodigious, step

Around a pile of mountains,
And, supercilious, peer
In shanties by the sides of roads,
And then a quarry pare

To fit its sides, and crawl between,
Complaining all the while
In horrid, hooting stanza,
Then chase itself down hill

And neigh like Boanerges—
Then, punctual as a star,
Stop—docile and omnipotent—
At its own stable door.

Emily Dickinson

"Aha!" cried the boy. "You talk, and I know what you say! Once you were a tiny seed—a papoose wrapped in white down. Your cradleboard swung from a twig. Then a strong Summer Wind came by. He lifted you from your mother's arms and brought you here. You see," laughed the boy, "I understand tree-talk! And I think he was a wise Wind. He planted your seed in this mud among sharp-edged rocks, where buffalo do not like to walk. But soon now they will reach over the rocks to scratch themselves against your branches. I'll make a stockade to protect you!" And the boy piled rocks higher around the lone sapling.

That is the beginning of 200 years of watching and wondering for the tree.

Uri Shulevitz has written and illustrated marvelous picture books, especially folk tales. As he states in his entry in *Contemporary Authors*, "Realizing the excess of words in our culture, I followed an Oriental tradition, trying to say more with fewer words." One of his books that has only brief text but wonderful words is *Dawn*. In this book he illustrates the change from the darkness of night to the blues of dawn until the sun changes the blue water to green. He describes the sounds and the visual image as two fishermen go out to fish: "The oars screak and rattle,/churning pools of foam." This would be a good book to share as you introduce students to haiku (see Chapter 4).

Thinking + Lesson Plan 6 in Appendix A (see page 147) focuses on the metaphor contained in Emily Dickinson's poem "I Like to See It Lap the Miles," which appears on the opposite page.

The following poem contains another excellent example of an extended metaphor to share with students. When using Thinking + Lesson Plan 6, give students plenty of time to consider possibilities for their metaphors. Share those that students discover as a way of stimulating the thinking of others.

Smoke Animals
Out of the factory chimney tall
Great black animals like to crawl.
They push each other and shove and crowd.
They nose the wind and they claw a cloud.
And they walk right out on the empty sky
With their tails all curled and their heads held high.
Rowena Bastin Bennett

Observing Other Literary Matters

There are many other literary elements that we can help students observe. As they read, and as they try to create literature, they will benefit from discussion of topics such as characterization, plot development, story beginnings and endings, and point of view.

Characterization

Many picture book authors develop a strong sense of characters. One example is Sam Cornish's character of a grandmother created through both text and pictures in *Grandmother's Pictures*, illustrated by Jeanne Johns. You meet the grandmother through her grandson's eyes. Then one day, she introduces her grandson to the other members of his family through the pictures and clippings she has collected over the years. After reading this sensitive story, you realize that it is the grandson who has been most clearly developed through his relationship with his grandmother and then his reaction to the pictures she shares, particularly those of his father who died when the boy was young. The black and white illustrations in this book are especially insightful. This is a wonderful picture of an African American family's life in an earlier time.

As mentioned earlier in this chapter, Florence Heide's story *Sound of Sunshine, Sound of Rain* has much to offer as a teaching tool. You may have to search for this book, but it is well worth the effort. The author develops the characters of a boy and his older sister skillfully. You have to read carefully to learn that the main character is a boy; student teachers have missed this important detail when I read it aloud. Also, he is blind, a fact that is shown, not told, through the boy's behavior and his sister's words, so there is much to be learned through inference. It is the sister as a character that I find most interesting. She is portrayed as sharp and impatient; the boy describes her heels as "like scissors cutting holes in my mother's voice." One significant scene provides empathy for this young African American woman. In a store the sister and brother have entered, another shopper remarks about their color. The siblings leave the store immediately.

"So we're colored," says my sister to me as she pulls me along. "So what else is new? I've heard it a million times. I guess I heard it before I was even born."

"Abram says color don't mean a thing," I say.

My sister drags me along. I can tell by her hand that she's mad. "What does he know? Is he black, your friend?" she asks.

"I don't know," I say.

"You don't even know if your friend is black or not," says my sister. "I wish everyone in the whole world was blind!" she cries.

After reading this book aloud, ask the students the following questions to guide them to greater understanding:

1. Who tells this story? (point of view)

2. Who are the characters in this story? (boy; sister; Abram, the philosophical ice cream man; woman in the store; the mother who is always off-stage) Notice that no one has a name except Abram.

3. Did you like the sister? What changed your mind about her?

4. How do you know the boy is blind?

5. Where did this story take place? (setting—city, perhaps Boston) A clue: The boy drinks water from a bubbler.

6. When did the story take place? (setting—perhaps 30 years ago) A clue: The young blind boy goes to a city park for hours alone, which he could not do today; also the use of the word "colored." Tell the students when the book was published.

Plot Development

Many picture books can be used to help students become aware of plot development. The chief advantage of the picture book is its brevity. You can read a story in 15 to 20 minutes and still have time to discuss the plot.

One fine book to use to introduce a lesson about plot development is the folk tale *Hansel and Gretel*, translated from the German writings of Jakob and Wilhelm Grimm by Elizabeth D. Crawford and illustrated by Lisbeth Zwerger. This is a particularly attractive edition of this tale with lovely sepia-toned ink and wash pictures. Read the story aloud to the class, and then guide them to map out the story something like the example on the next page.

When students read a story independently, they can construct a map similar to the example for *Hansel and Gretel* to analyze how the author developed the tale. When they plan to write a story, they might map the elements of the story in the same way. Different ways of mapping can be invented. A time line provides an excellent kind of map for an autobiography or biography.

Beginning and Ending a Story

Have students compare how different authors begin their stories. Sherry Garland begins her simple tale of an immigrant from Vietnam this way: "My

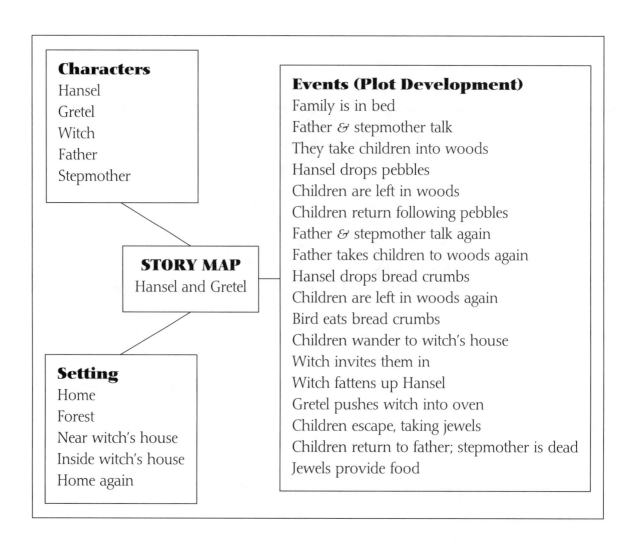

Characters
Hansel
Gretel
Witch
Father
Stepmother

STORY MAP
Hansel and Gretel

Setting
Home
Forest
Near witch's house
Inside witch's house
Home again

Events (Plot Development)
Family is in bed
Father & stepmother talk
They take children into woods
Hansel drops pebbles
Children are left in woods
Children return following pebbles
Father & stepmother talk again
Father takes children to woods again
Hansel drops bread crumbs
Children are left in woods again
Bird eats bread crumbs
Children wander to witch's house
Witch invites them in
Witch fattens up Hansel
Gretel pushes witch into oven
Children escape, taking jewels
Children return to father; stepmother is dead
Jewels provide food

grandmother saw/the emperor cry/the day he lost/his golden dragon throne." Her poetic text and Tatsuro Kiuchi's gorgeous paintings combine to create a beautiful book, *The Lotus Seed*. The ending of this story refers to the opening sentence, as the narrator of the tale thinks about telling her own children "about the day my grandmother saw the emperor cry." This type of beginning and ending forms a circle as readers return to the same spot where they began.

Donald Crews begins his story of an extended African American family with questions: "Did you see her? Did you see Bigmama?" He continues his story *Bigmama's* by explaining that Bigmama is the name given his Mama's Mama. The family is setting out to visit her as they do every summer. The ending of this book is unusual, too, because on the final page a grown man is remembering the annual visits to Bigmama's: "Some nights even now, I think that I might wake up in the morning and be at Bigmama's with the whole summer ahead of me."

Students can compare other endings. In *Hansel and Gretel*, as discussed in the previous section, for example, the author writes the final sentence and then adds a stylized story ending that might be fun for students to try in their own writing:

Then all their troubles were at an end, and they lived together in complete happiness.

My tale is done, and there a mouse does run. Whoever catches it can make a big fur cap of it.

Have students prepare a bulletin board display labeled "Beginnings" and "Endings," where they can mount copies of interesting examples they have collected from stories. Have students share their contributions orally, and discuss the varied ways authors begin and end stories. Students might compare the different examples, selecting one or more that they prefer.

Exploring Point of View

Students seem to enjoy writing stories that are told from different points of view. They can use picture books as models for writing original point of view tales that usually prove to be very funny. Following are several picture books to use as models.

A story with an unusual point of view is *Voices in the Park* by Anthony Browne. Only the pictures reveal the humor inherent in Browne's portrayal of the characters as members of the monkey family who otherwise behave as humans, living in houses, owning dogs to take to the park, and wearing human clothing. Students may observe some inaccuracy in the author/illustrator's drawing of the characters because the adults look like gorillas and the two children look more like young chimpanzees. However, the tale is a marvelous example of point of view of a mother and then a father followed by the woman's son and the father's daughter. The two children meet in the park and so do the two dogs. They have a wonderful time while the parents sit thinking on their respective park benches. Their individual summaries of what happened in the park are quite amusing.

Authors like Jon Scieszka have had fun rewriting familiar tales, taking liberties to tickle our funny bones. In *The True Story of The 3 Little Pigs by A. Wolf*, mentioned earlier, he has the wolf tell what really happened. As he relates the tale, it all happened because he had a terrible sneezy cold, and he was making a cake for his dear old granny and ran out of sugar. Naturally, he went to his neighbor's house to borrow the sugar. The neighbor had built his house of straw, a really silly thing to do, so when he knocked on the door, it fell in. The dusty straw caused him to begin to sneeze; he huffed and snuffed and sneezed a big sneeze which caused the house to fall apart. Your students will love this story, and they may be inspired to try rewriting a tale themselves.

Perspective, a little different from point of view, can be introduced with the book *Something Beautiful*, written by Sharon Dennis Wyeth and illustrated by Chris K. Soentpiet. A young African American girl looks out her city window and sees nothing but ugliness—an old homeless woman sleeping in a cardboard box, garbage in the courtyard, and nasty graffiti on the building door. Then, her teacher teaches the students the word *beautiful*, something that makes you happy, so she writes the word in her notebook and sets out to find something beautiful. As she meets her friends, she asks them what they have that is beautiful. She sees her aunt with her baby in the launderette. As she tickles the laughing baby, her aunt says, "My baby's laugh is something *beautiful*." So she heads home to remove some of the ugliness by washing the graffiti off the door and beginning to pick up the garbage. When her mother comes home from work, she asks if she has something beautiful. "Of course," her mother replies, "I have you." A nice sense of an urban community is depicted sensitively by the artist.

Studying Myths and Legends

Students at the secondary level should become familiar with the myths and legends that permeate our literature and language. Beautiful picture books present many stories from Greek, Roman, and Norse mythology as well as tales about national heroes.

Artist and illustrator Hudson Talbott has specialized in the legends around King Arthur and his knights. One such title is *Excalibur* in which he tells the story of young Arthur's quests as King of Britain. This tale focuses on Arthur's fight with a rebellious warrior, King Pellinore. Talbott's latest book is *Lancelot: Tales of King Arthur*. He also wrote and illustrated *King Arthur: The Sword in the Stone* and *King Arthur and the Round Table*. These tales focus on the days of chivalry and great heroes, which students usually enjoy. The books are illustrated handsomely with splashy double-page spreads that add much to the excitement of the adventures.

The mightiest of the Greek heroes is featured in *The Twelve Labors of Hercules*, written by James Riordan and illustrated by Christina Balit. The mortal Hercules performs great feats. When he is killed by a jealous woman, he is taken to live on Mt. Olympus with his father, Zeus. Students might compare this edition with *The Twelve Labors of Hercules*, retold by Robert Newman and illustrated by Charles

Keeping. Nancy Loewen also wrote and illustrated *Hercules*. Robert Burleigh chose to feature only the final, most difficult task in *Hercules*, illustrated by Colon Raul.

The following picture books suggest other topics of interest related to the Greek and Roman myths:

Athena by Nancy Loewen. At the end of this book the author compares the Greek and Roman gods and goddesses.

Daughter of Earth: A Roman Myth by George McDermott. Here is the story of Proserpine whose mother, Ceres, tries to save her from Pluto, god of the under-world.

Romulus and Remus by Anne F. Rockwell. This author presents the fascinating tale of the twin boys, raised by a wolf, who were the founders of Rome.

Typical of the great national epics is India's *Mahabharata*. A tale from this folk-lore is *Savitri: A Tale of Ancient India*, written by Aaron Shepard and illustrated by Vera Rosenberry. In this tale a princess outwits the god of death to save her hus-band. Uma Krishnaswami relates the story of *The Broken Tusk: Stories of the Hindu God Ganesha*, illustrated by Maniam Selven. This collection centers on the "some-times greedy, sometimes impulsive, but always generous" elephant-headed Ganesha. Another collection of stories from India's mythology is *The Adventures of Young Krishna: The Blue God of India*, retold and illustrated by Diksha Dalal-Clayton.

Students can conduct research about the mythology of any country or re-gion. Begin by brainstorming all the possible topics or subjects they can generate from their shared knowledge. As they search, they may find more topics. Students can begin searching the local library's catalog, which may be available on com-puter. Turning to other sites on the Internet, they might explore book publishers, the American Library Association, or the Library of Congress.

Conclusion

In Chapter 5 we have investigated such topics as the history of English and I have introduced other languages, including sign. I chose to look at poetry study in this chapter as well as various other genres, for example, the fable and parody. I also included a section on imagery and such literary devices as point of view and story structure, including characterization. The chapter concluded with a fo-cus on myths and legends. In Chapter 6 we will address the important study of di-versity in our multiculture.

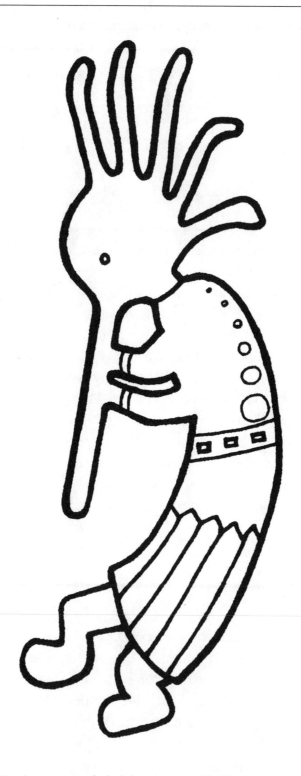

Kokopelli—Native American symbol of abundance and fertility

CHAPTER 6

Understanding and Appreciating Diversity

In the United States we are all part of a multiculture comprising many diverse people: young and old, big and little, dark skinned and light skinned, people of different ethnic and racial backgrounds, and people expressing different beliefs. In each classroom we see this diversity represented.

Picture books can help us teach multiculturally as we guide students toward greater understanding and appreciation of the other students in their classes. The ideas in this chapter follow the model suggested by Pamela Tiedt and me in the fifth edition of *Multicultural Teaching* (1999). We believe that appreciation begins with a feeling of self-worth or esteem for each individual, which can be extended to others as empathy and lead to equity for all. Selected picture books can be used to promote understanding of diversity and to achieve these goals as we work with middle school students. Enlarge the figure on the facing page to feature on a display about diversity.

Supporting Esteem for Each Individual

Especially important during the adolescent years is support for each student's self-esteem. It is never too late to give students the appreciation they need.

Learning About Self-Esteem

Students need to understand what esteem is and how it affects our lives. Talk about self-esteem with students: What does it mean to have self-esteem? How might you hurt someone's feelings and possibly their self-esteem? Bring in picture books to initiate discussion of this important topic.

Mary Hoffman has written and illustrated a wonderful story that focuses on self-esteem, *Amazing Grace*. A young African American, Grace, wants to play the part of Peter Pan in a school production. Everyone tells her she can't be Peter Pan because she is a girl, and, further, Peter Pan is not African American. Nevertheless, she auditions for the part and dances so wonderfully that she gets the part.

Anthony Browne presents an interesting character in *Willy the Wimp*. Everyone makes fun of Willy, and the big guys pick on him. All Willy replies is, "I'm sorry." Then, he decides to fight back by taking a body building course. At last, he is big and strong enough to rescue his friend Millie from street bullies. In the final scene our "hero" walks proudly with his head in the air, straight into a pole. Willy says, "I'm sorry." This humorous story should generate interesting discussion. The fact that the characters are animals may make the story and its theme less threatening. Develop a lesson as described in Thinking + Lesson Plan 8 in Appendix A (see page 149).

Additional books that deal with self-esteem include *Paperboy* by Mary Kay Kroeger and Louise Borden, which tells the story of a newsboy in Cincinnati, Ohio, in 1927 when Tunney and Dempsey are fighting for the world heavyweight boxing championship. The night of the fight Willie Brinkman is the first boy to pick up his papers, but he cannot sell a single paper. Despite his discouragement, Willie picks up his papers the next night as usual and is rewarded for his perseverance by being assigned to the best corner in the city. Illustrations by Ted Lewin depict Cincinnati's urban setting in the 1920s.

Munro Leaf's classic tale *The Story of Ferdinand* describes a bull who prefers to smell the flowers rather than fight. However, Ferdinand suddenly appears to be a ferocious bull when a bee stings him, and he becomes a hero. This well-told funny story set in Spain is illustrated with exceptionally fine black and white drawings by Robert Lawson.

When Agnes Caws, written by Candace Fleming and illustrated by Giselle Potter, tells the story of an 8-year-old who is a world-renowned birdcaller. She is sent to the Himalayas to locate a pink-headed duck; there she tangles with Colonel Pittsnap who wants to find the rare duck himself. Agnes is definitely in charge.

Sharing such books invites discussion about the way people feel. Give each cooperative learning group one book to read and discuss. Each group will share what they learned from the book they read.

Solving Personal Problems

Many students have difficulty dealing with emotions they feel and problems they face. Introduce discussion about different emotions that we all experience. You might begin with *When Sophie Gets Angry—Really, Really Angry*, written and illustrated by Molly Bang. If you stop reading before Sophie calms down, middle school students can readily evaluate Sophie's angry behavior. There may be discussion about whether Sophie has a right to become angry when "her sister grabbed the gorilla." Students might talk in small groups about times they have experienced anger, then write in their individual journals about their discussions. Afterward, finish the book that shows how Sophie gets over her anger and returns home happy. Again, students can talk about what they do after they get mad.

What kinds of problems do your students experience? How do we solve our problems? A number of picture books will help to introduce aspects of this topic for discussion. Following are examples of books that address personal problems that some middle school students must deal with.

Lying. A Quaker boy faces the problem of lying in *The Adventures of Obadiah* by Brinton Turkle. Another book that treats this problem is *Sam, Bangs, and Moonshine*, written and illustrated by Evaline Ness. This book won the Caldecott Award with its wonderful drawings that enhance the story of Samantha, who could tell wilder stories than all the sailors "home from the sea." Another intriguing twist to the problem of lying is given by humorist Hilaire Belloc in *Matilda, Who Told Lies, and Was Burned to Death*. Illustrated by Posy Simmonds, this tale is about a girl who got her "just desserts," a take-off on the story of "The Boy Who Cried Wolf."

Being afraid. Kevin Henkes introduces a serious problem in *Owen*. A young mouse is afraid to begin school without his tattered security blanket. A similar story is presented in Bernard Waber's *Ira Sleeps Over* in which a little boy cannot go to sleep at a friend's house without his favorite teddy bear. Students can talk about times when they were afraid. This is a good writing subject.

Missing parents. Charlotte Zolotow addresses the problem faced by a child who has no father in *A Father Like That*. Introducing such stories to older students may help them talk or write about problems they face dealing with divorced or deceased parents. Such discussion may be easier in small groups in which students do not feel so exposed.

Being illiterate. Patricia Polacco tells a poignant autobiographical story in *Thank You, Mr. Falker*. Trisha, the youngest child in the family depicted, fully expects to learn to read when she enters school. Her older brothers share their books with her, and her schoolteacher mother reads aloud to her. She loves books, and she loves school, mostly because she can draw there. Other children are learning to read, but not Trisha. Reading is a struggle for her, and her classmates tease her. However, by listening carefully and memorizing, she manages to fool teachers into thinking that she can read. Then, a new teacher, Mr. Falker, admires her artistic talents, and he scolds the children who make fun of her. But most important, he recognizes Trisha's problem and begins tutoring her after school. Slowly she acquires the skills she needs, and suddenly she can read a whole sentence, then a paragraph. Years later she thanked Mr. Falker for his help. "What do you do?" he asked. Patricia Polacco answered, "I make books for children. Thank you, Mr. Falker."

We don't always know the problems students face. It is important that somehow, somewhere, they have a chance to talk about them.

Developing Empathy for Others

One of the most important results of interactive learning is the development of *empathy* for other students. Working in cooperative learning groups students come to know each other's strengths and foibles. They learn civility and tolerance for differing opinions and beliefs, and they learn to work together to achieve a common goal. They learn to function as a family and as a community of scholars. Picture books can be used to teach explicit lessons about getting along with others in a classroom, in a community, and in a country.

Welcoming Newcomers

In most schools there is increasing diversity, including children for whom English is a second language. Picture books can introduce discussion about the problems these students and others face as they enter a new school.

The struggles of a young Spanish-speaking Latino, Francisco, as he enters a school in the United States are presented realistically in *La Mariposa* by Francisco Jimenez. Illustrated by Simon Silva, this story introduces some Spanish, which can usually be understood in the context of the action. (A glossary is included.) The title refers to the monarch butterfly that is the only thing this non–English-speaking child can relate to at first. Francisco's drawing of the butterfly wins a blue ribbon and recognition by his classmates. Although the character is younger than middle school students, they can discuss how Francisco felt—lonely, isolated, and unhappy. Compile a list of these adjectives on the chalkboard. Then ask students to choose one of the feelings and to describe, in groups or in writing, an incident that caused them to feel as Francisco does in the story.

The classic story about Chibi, an outsider who sits silently in the classroom, is presented in *Crow Boy*, written and illustrated by Taro Yashima. A new teacher talks with Chibi and learns that he walks many miles to school each day. He knows much about the plants of the countryside, and he can imitate the calls of the crows. After he demonstrates this ability to the amazement of the children, they call him Crow Boy and accept him as a member of the group. Yashima presents an important message without moralizing, so the book provides an outstanding stimulus for discussion.

A charming story is told by John Archambault in *Grandmother's Garden*. In grandmother's garden, we are all one: "Earth is a garden turning 'round the sun,/With room to bloom for everyone." Students need to think about how they can reach out to befriend others. They also may consider how important friends are in their own lives as they work with the lesson in Thinking + Lesson Plan 9 in Appendix A (see page 150).

Developing the Theme of Friendship

Friendship is a marvelous theme to develop with students in the middle school. Peer relations are particularly important at this time as they move into adolescence. The theme ties in well with the development of empathy for others.

Picture books that would be appropriate for developing the theme of friendship include the following:

The Malachite Palace, written by Alma Flor Ada and illustrated by Leonid Gore. In this fairy tale a young princess has everything that should make her happy. But she doesn't have a friend. Outside the palace she sees children laughing and playing, but the adults tell her they are rude and ignorant. One day her attendants capture a tiny yellow bird that flies into the garden, but it will not sing. Finally, the princess puts the bird cage on the balcony, and it sings in response to the children's laughter below. At last the princess frees the bird and joins the laughing children.

Everett Anderson's Friend by Lucille Clifton. Everett is disappointed to find that his new neighbor is a girl, but his feelings change when he discovers that she is a good ball player.

I Like You, If You Like Me: Poems of Friendship, edited by Myra Cohn Livingstone.

Chicken Sunday by Patricia Polacco. Two African American boys and a friend (the author as a girl) earn money to buy their grandmother an Easter hat.

For Pete's Sake by Ellen Stoll Walsh. This author presents a simple story that older students could share with elementary-grade children. Pete is an alligator who wonders why he does not look like the flamingos he meets. They suggest that he probably just is not ripe yet because he is green. Then Pete discovers he has four feet and the friendly flamingos have only two. They tell him he is lucky because he has two extra feet. Finally, Pete meets other alligators who look just like him. "Pete almost popped with joy." He tells his flamingo friends that he is different and the same. They reply, "Well, for Pete's sake, Pete.…You always have been."

Real Events Related to Diversity

Picture books can help introduce events in U.S. history that are directly related to the study of diversity. For example, the topic of the internment of Japanese Americans during World War II is dealt with in Eve Bunting's *So Far From the Sea*. The author writes simply about a Japanese American family that has been affected both directly and indirectly by the internment. Before moving to Massachusetts, the family visits the grandfather's grave at Manzanar in southern California to say good-bye. Chris Soentpiet's black and white illustrations help the reader understand what internment was like. He uses color to portray what still remains at Manzanar today to remind us of this injustice.

Another picture book that introduces the internment experience is *The Bracelet* by Yoshiko Uchida. Emi's friend, Laurie, gives her a friendship bracelet just before Emi's Japanese American family leaves for a relocation center. (This picture book could introduce the study of Uchida's novel *Journey to Topaz*.)

Another memorable event in U.S. history is the integration of the public schools and the end of segregation. Robert Coles relates the story of one of the first African American children to enter an all-white school in *The Story of Ruby Bridges*. George Ford's illustrations help readers understand Ruby's experience as she enters first grade in William Frantz Elementary School. Students could research other stories of the first African American students in desegregated schools, discovering what happened to them as they grew up. One of them, for example, is Melba Beals, who became a noted journalist and author.

Eve Bunting wrote an interesting story about a night of riots like those in Los Angeles, California, in 1992. *Smoky Night* paints a realistic and frightening picture of this urban scene—fire, smashed windows, and looting. David Diaz won the Caldecott Award for his vivid illustrations in this book; he uses varied media to achieve striking effects. The story focuses on two cats who never got along. After the riots, however, a firefighter finds them huddled together. Somehow the frightening happenings seem to have affected them positively, and suddenly they are drinking milk from the same dish in the shelter where the neighbors have gathered. Like the people in the neighborhood, their fright has made them forget their differences.

Getting to Know Different Cultures

People are more alike than they are different. Reading stories can help to make this concept clear to children of all ages. For instance, in Phil Mendez's story *The Black Snowman*, Jacob Miller is disillusioned, tired of being poor, and tired of everything black, even the sooty snow. Nonetheless, he helps his little brother, Pee Wee, build a black snowman, which suddenly speaks out. When Pee Wee is caught in a burning building, the snowman melts as he helps Jacob save the younger boy. It is then that Jacob begins to understand what is important in life.

The meaning of the Jewish celebration of the Seder is explained in simple, poetic language with detailed illustrations in *This Is Our Seder*, written by Ziporah Hildebrandt and illustrated by Robin Roraback. This kind of book must be examined closely in order to read the illustrations that can be summarized orally or written in descriptive paragraphs. A one-page overview of Passover traditions provides helpful information. This is only one fine picture book that helps non-Jewish students understand the beliefs of the Jewish people. Mark Podwal tells *The Menorah Story*, which non-Jews also will find enlightening. Other picture books about Jewish people and their beliefs include the following:

A Picture Book of Hanukkah by David Adler

Ben Goes Into Business by Marilyn Hirsh

The Sign on Mendel's Window by Mildred Phillips

The Story of Hanukkah, written by Amy Ehrlich and illustrated by Ori Sherman

Many picture books relate stories about African American children and their families. An especially fine example is Tony Johnston's *The Wagon*, illustrated with beautiful paintings by James Ransome. This autobiographical presentation tells a slave child's rebellious thoughts from birth to freedom. When he is 12, his family sets off in the handsome wagon his father had made as a slave to participate in U.S. President Abraham Lincoln's funeral.

A narrative about a real African American is told and illustrated by William Miller in *Richard Wright and the Library Card*, a book mentioned in Chapter 3. William Miller also wrote a touching story *Zora Hurston and the Chinaberry Tree*, illustrated by Cornelius Van Wright and Ying-Hwa Hu, about another African American writer, Zora Neale Hurston, whose mother encouraged her to reach for what she wanted. Her mother also made Zora listen to the stories the people told and made her promise to remember them. When Zora's mother became ill and died, Zora remembered her promise and her mother's encouragement as she climbed high in the chinaberry tree.

Another attractive book that may interest your students is *Cornrows* by Camille Yarbrough, illustrated by Carole Byard. Look for books by Faith Ringgold described in Chapter 8 and those illustrated by African American artist Jerry Pinkney, for example, *The Talking Eggs* by Robert D. San Souci.

Providing Equity for Everyone

You might discuss with students the difference between equality and equity. The phrase we often hear, "All people are created equal," can be confusing. Not all persons are equal in ability, for example, but we can provide equitable treatment for people of all abilities, giving each individual the equal opportunity to achieve to his or her greatest potential. In this section I address a few major concerns relating to equity and suggest picture books you can use to introduce the topics to students.

Exploring Stereotyped Thinking

Stereotyped thinking is a common problem that we can address with middle school students. We can focus on both female and male stereotypes as well as stereotyped thinking about the elderly. An interesting way to introduce this topic is to consider first stereotypes about animals, for example, the wolf.

Stereotypes of animals. Talking about stereotyped ideas about animals is less threatening than is discussing stereotyped thinking about people. You can use the lesson in Thinking + Lesson Plan 10 in Appendix A (see page 151) to introduce a study about stereotyped thinking.

Picture books about wolves that you might look for to use in Thinking + Lesson Plan 10 include the following:

Wolf!, written by Becky Bloom and illustrated by Pascal Biet. In this book a hungry wolf does not frighten the barnyard animals even when he growls threateningly. They tell him to "Be big and dangerous somewhere else and stop bothering us while we're reading. This is a farm for educated animals." So, the wolf learns to read and with expression!

The True Story of The 3 Little Pigs by A. Wolf by Jon Scieszka. Mentioned earlier, this is a delightful different point of view of the traditional tale.

Howling Hill, written by Will Hobbs and illustrated by Jill Kastner. This story of a wolf family presents a positive image of real wolves living together. While playing with her brothers and sisters, young Hanni is swept away on a log in the river. Lost and lonely, she scrambles out of the water and gets help from a friendly bear who guides her back toward Howling Hill and her family.

Once a Wolf: How Wildlife Biologists Fought to Bring Back the Gray Wolf, written by Stephen Swinburne with photographs by Jim Brandenburg. This is an excellent overview of the relationship between humans and wolves and clarification of "the difference between the wolf of legend and the wolf of fact." Includes Web sites for additional information.

Yo, Hungry Wolf!, written by David Vozar and illustrated by Betsy Lewin. This is a truly funny story that tells the wolf's story in rap with pictures that will delight your students. The poor wolf meets Red Rappinghood who sees through his disguise in a minute, three gutsy pigs that he can't frighten, and finally, the boy who cried wolf too late.

Female stereotypes. Of concern today is the image of women in children's literature. The following picture books treat this subject either directly or indirectly.

The Legend of the White Buffalo Woman by Paul Goble. The author presents a strong female figure from Native American mythology. It was the White Buffalo Woman who brought the peace pipe to the Lakota nation. These Plains Indians came annually to quarry pipestone in what is now a national monument in southern Minnesota.

Women of Hope: African Americans Who Made a Difference by Joyce Hansen. This book features 14 biographies of women such as Maya Angelou, the Delany sisters, and Marian Wright Edelman. Additional women are listed in the Appendix.

Brave Margaret: An Irish Adventure, written by Robert D. San Souci and illustrated by Sally Wern Comport. Redheaded and Irish, brave Margaret manages to break down traditional stereotypes as she banishes a sea serpent, slays the wicked giant, and saves her prince's life. The book is illustrated beautifully.

Hurry, Hurry, Mary Dear, written by N.M. Bodecker and illustrated by Erik Blegvad. This humorous poem depicts the common stereotype of the husband's giving orders to his wife. The final illustration shows him getting his just desserts: the teapot of hot tea he had just demanded from his exhausted wife over his head!

When Mama Comes Home Tonight, written by Eileen Spinelli and illustrated by Jane Dyer. Handsome paintings support the poetic language in this book as we see a working mother return home to love her child. This is another wonderful model for creating original books.

Male stereotypes. Men characters too can be stereotyped. Today a number of authors attempt to portray men more positively as fathers.

My Daddy by Susan Paradis. This charming story tells of a young boy's admiration for his father. Wonderful illustrations by the author serve to break down the stereotype of the absent father. This is an excellent model for the creation of children's books suggested in Chapter 8, and it could be used with the theme of love discussed in Chapter 9.

Kevin and His Dad, written by Irene Smalls and illustrated by Michael Hays. Kevin and his dad share a Saturday working and playing while Mother is away and delight in each other's company. As Kevin says, "I love being with my dad; he's the best friend a guy ever had."

As the Crow Flies, written by Elizabeth Winthrop and illustrated by Joan Sandin. The child of divorced parents, Michael lives in Arizona with his mother while his father lives in Delaware. His father stays in a motel when he comes to visit, and Michael naturally feels sad when his dad returns to Delaware. Finally, however, the parents decide that he is old enough to fly alone to Delaware, "two thousand miles as the crow flies," to spend the whole summer. The author speaks clearly to children who share the experience of divorce.

African Americans. Realistic stories about family life of people from different cultures help to break down stereotypes. One of the earliest picture books about African American families is John Steptoe's *Stevie*. Colorful illustrations support this story of Robert, who resents having Stevie stay temporarily with his family. When Stevie is no longer with them, however, Robert realizes that he misses the little boy. Also illustrated by Steptoe is another portrayal of family life featuring African Americans, Eloise Greenfield's *She Come Bringing Me That Little Baby Girl*.

In this realistic story a little boy resents having a baby sister rather than a brother, but he learns to appreciate her. Another classic, Ezra Jack Keats's *The Snowy Day*, tells of a young boy's enchantment with snow. (See Chapter 8 for more information about this book.) These books focus on the lives of the characters presented, not the color of their skin. First read aloud one of the stories without showing students the illustrations. Then have students draw and color a picture of the main character. Compare the many differences in how individuals pictured these people. Then tell the students, "This is how the author and illustrator pictured this character," and show them the illustrations. Discuss the effect of the illustrations on their feelings about the characters.

Slavery is a topic of historical interest and a theme that could be explored in some detail. Many fine picture books provide pertinent information and illustrations that are sometimes much more poignant than traditional textbooks. In *Follow the Drinking Gourd*, for example, Jeanette Winter tells the story of Peg Leg Joe's ways of helping slaves escape to freedom by looking up to find the North Star. Winter's handsome illustrations enhance this historically accurate story. A second story that contrasts the lives of white and black people on the plantations in the southern United States is *Christmas in the Big House; Christmas in the Quarters*, written by Patricia McKissack and Fredrick McKissack and illustrated by John Thompson. This is a beautiful book that students can use to compare lives of the master and his family with that of the slaves who worked for them. Stories about real people add new dimensions to history, for example, *Minty: A Story of Young Harriet Tubman*, written by Alan Schroeder and illustrated by Jerry Pinkney. Her dream of gaining freedom was all that made life on the plantation tolerable for 8-year-old Minty who was considered a "problem slave" by her master.

Not all Africans came to America as slaves. Walter Dean Myers wrote *Amistad: A Long Road to Freedom* to tell the tale of African men who were captured but never became slaves. Captured in Africa, they turned against the captain and took over the ship Amistad. Imprisoned in the United States, these leaders fought successfully for their freedom in the courts and were eventually returned to their homes. This story was presented as a film in 1997, directed by Steven Spielberg.

The elderly. Students may have stereotyped views of the elderly, particularly if they are not close to any old people. *How Does It Feel to Be Old?* is the title of Norma Farber's poetic response to this important question posed by a granddaughter. Illustrated by Trina Schart Hyman, this book could introduce a study of the aged in society, beginning with those closest to us. In *Wilfrid Gordon McDonald Partridge*, illustrated by Julie Vivas, Australian author Mem Fox gives another perspective of aging through the eyes of a young boy and his friends who live in an "old people's home." Wilfrid has many friends, but his favorite is Miss Nancy who has lost her memory. He learns what memory is as he strives to find hers for her.

Patricia Polacco's *Mrs. Katz and Tush* is a marvelous story of the friendship between a young African American boy and an old Jewish woman. Tush is the kitten the boy gives to Mrs. Katz to keep her company.

Song and Dance Man, written by Karen Ackerman and illustrated by Stephen Gammell, won the Caldecott Award. In this story the grandfather, who was once a "song and dance" man, performs for his grandchildren. He is exhausted, but they're delighted, and they see grandpa in a different light.

Cooperating at Home and in the Community

As we deal with diversity in the classroom, we can emphasize learning to get along with others.

Family

Most students have jobs to do within the family. Introduce a discussion of such responsibilities by reading a book like Eve Bunting's *The Wednesday Surprise*. In this story a young girl secretly teaches her elderly grandmother to read. Muriel Stanek addresses a similar problem for families who have just immigrated to the United States in *I Speak English for My Mom*, illustrated by Judith Friedman. Illiteracy is also the subject of Ruth Yaffe Radin's *All Joseph Wanted*, illustrated by Deborah Kogan Ray. Joseph's mother cannot read until he convinces her to enroll in an adult literacy class.

Community

Leo Lionni tells the story of a fish community in *Swimmy*. In this classic tale the little fish are threatened by a huge fish. Led by Swimmy, the little fish unite to form an even bigger fish that frightens away their common enemy. Lionni's illustrations provide beautiful underwater scenes. This is also an excellent example of problem solving.

Thomas F. Yezerski describes friction between two ethnic groups within a village in *Together in Pinecone Patch*. Immigrants from Ireland and Poland bring their prejudices with them as they arrive in a small Pennsylvania coal-mining town. Keara and Stefan show the community that what they share is much more important than their differences. The Irish and Polish immigrants join together to celebrate this couple's wedding.

Conflict, Violence, and War

The Cello of Mr. O, written by Jane Cutler and illustrated by Greg Couch, tells a story of the effects of war in the words of a young girl. Mr. O, a neighbor who had never been friendly, demonstrates great courage as he sits in the plaza playing his cello to comfort the frightened people during a bombing raid. When his beautiful cello is ruined, he continues to play on a small harmonica.

The Butter Battle Book by Dr. Seuss tells a funny, yet serious story about war. This book could generate a discussion about war and how it begins.

Conclusion

In this chapter we have discussed teaching multiculturally with an emphasis on developing students' feelings of esteem, empathy for others, and equity for all. I presented the theme of friendship as an example of the kinds of studies that help build a sense of community in the classroom. In particular I emphasized an examination of stereotyped thinking with middle school students as it relates to gender, age, and different cultures. In Chapter 7 we will look at picture books that can help us develop studies in the social studies, mathematics, and science curricula.

Illustration from *Baba Yaga* by Blair Lent. Illustrations copyright ©1966 by Blair Lent, Jr., renewed 1994 by Blair Lent. Reprinted by permission of Houghton Mifflin Company. All rights reserved.

CHAPTER 7

Crossing the Curriculum

Picture books have much to offer teachers and students in any subject area. In this chapter I limit the discussion to the use of these books in social studies, science, and mathematics. Using picture books in art and music is addressed in Chapter 8. The emphasis, as elsewhere in this text, is on integrating the language arts and reading with content areas across the curriculum. Because the total number of books to be considered is enormous, what is presented here is just a sampling of ideas for you to develop with your students.

Introducing Topics in the Social Studies

Some of the most exciting picture books present topics relating to history and geography. Quality illustrations add much to presentations about topics in history, often producing informational books that were never intended for use with preschool and primary-grade children. The illustrations in these books should prove fascinating to middle school students.

Around the World With Picture Books

Around the World: Who's Been Here?, written and illustrated by Lindsay Barrett George, contains letters written by a teacher to her students. Maps trace her route, and each letter is accompanied by large paintings depicting the wildlife she encounters. The author has written other books that focus on nature, for example, the woods, the pond, and the snow.

A Is for Asia, written by Cynthia Chin-Lee and illustrated by Yumi Heo, is a fascinating introduction to all of Asia. Interesting maps provide an overview of this part of the world. Each letter focuses attention on some aspect of life; for example, "*M* is for the *monsoon...*," and the author explains that farmers must hurry to finish planting before the rains begin. *R* is for *rice*, the grain that is eaten throughout Asia. This book could begin a class study focusing on Asia with small groups researching different countries.

A similar book, written by Cynthia Chin-Lee and Terri de la Peña and illustrated by Enrique O. Sánchez, is *A Is for the Americas*. Using the ABC format, the authors introduce concepts relating to the people in the Western Hemisphere. The emphasis is on Latinos and Native Americans. The book is available in Spanish.

An unusual collection of poetry, *The Space Between Our Footsteps: Poems and Paintings from the Middle East*, is presented by Naomi Shihab Nye. Nye shares her own story in Palestine as well as stories and art by poets and various talented artists. This book is an exciting way to explore the cultures of the Middle East.

Learning About Real People

Autobiographies and biographies offer one way of learning about real people and their contributions to society. Some students readily identify with life stories; it is information that inspires them or supports their sense of self-worth. Students also can use picture book biographies as models for reports on people of historical significance.

Contemporary figures may be of special interest to students. For example, ice skater Kristi Yamaguchi, with assistance from Greg Brown, wrote a charming autobiography titled *Always Dream*. Illustrated by Doug Keith, this attractive book contains many topics that can be used for teaching: Kristi's Japanese heritage, her love of family, and her struggle to achieve her dream.

An interesting companion to this skater's autobiography is the biography that Allen Say wrote and illustrated about his own grandfather's life: *Grandfather's Journey*. His grandfather, born in Japan, emigrated to California. However, he missed Japan, so he returned. Although he always talked about visiting California again, he never did.

Mr. Emerson's Cook, written and illustrated by Judith Schachner, is an unusual book. It could be presented under the poetry section in Chapter 5, but it also may be used when teaching history. The book is about how, as an early poet and philosopher, Ralph Waldo Emerson played an influential role in colonial society. The author has created a story that combines fantasy with fact in an engaging way that older students will find appealing.

Talented African American author Eloise Greenfield wrote a biography about early African American educator *Mary McLeod Bethune*. This volume is illustrated with black ink drawings by Jerry Pinkney. Greenfield also authored another title in this publisher's series, *Paul Robeson*, the story of the famous African American singer, illustrated by George Ford. Other biographies in this series of more than 30 titles focus on the lives of such people as Malcolm X, the Ringling Brothers, John Muir, Fannie Lou Hamer, Roberto Clemente, and Leonard Bernstein. These biographies are fairly traditional in presentation style. Look for other picture books by Eloise Greenfield, for example, *She Come Bringing Me That Little Baby Girl*.

Betsy Harvey Kraft used historical photographs to illustrate an interesting biography titled *Mother Jones: One Woman's Fight for Labor*. This energetic Irish immigrant fought for the rights of coal miners, and she was particularly concerned about the welfare of children who worked in textile mills. This book fits with gender studies as well as a study of the theme of immigrants and immigration.

Another author who has specialized in writing biographies for young people is David Adler. For example, he wrote *A Picture Book of Paul Revere*, illustrated by John and Alexandra Wallner. The text, brief but comprehensive, is extended nicely by the illustrations. Adler has written more than 25 of these "picture biographies," featuring such noted Americans as Martin Luther King, Helen Keller, Jackie Robinson, Sitting Bull, and Rosa Parks.

Jean Fritz has written several picture book biographies such as *You Want Women to Vote, Lizzie Stanton?*, illustrated by DyAnne DiSalvo-Ryan. This is an example of the feminist literature available for young people. Fritz also wrote *Harriet Beecher Stowe and the Beecher Preachers*. Some middle school students might like to explore the contributions of women in U.S. or world history. Look for other books by Jean Fritz, especially her young adult novels and her autobiographies.

An attractive biography by Rose Blue and Corinne J. Naden is *Colin Powell: Straight to the Top*. One in the Gateway Biography series, this book is illustrated with historical photographs from different sources. Students will notice that these authors choose to begin Powell's life story with his involvement in the Persian Gulf War when he was at the peak of his career. Students might observe how other biographers begin their books as a way of helping them improve their writing of biographical sketches. They may be surprised to find that few begin with the birth of the person.

Reading About Real Events

For some students, informative text is more engrossing than narrative text. Of course, there is always the element of story as we read about real events and the people who were involved, but good authors base their writing on careful research. Margy Burns Knight's *Talking Walls*, illustrated by Anne Sibley O'Brien, is an unusual collection of stories that touch on different events in world history. Can walls talk? What stories could they tell us? The author begins with the Great Wall of China and the story behind it. Each wall represents a culture and the history of a people. This book will motivate students to look at a globe of the world to locate each wall and to consider its surroundings. It opens up many discussion questions, suggesting a whole theme study as developed in Thinking + Lesson Plan 11 in Appendix A (see page 152). The author also has published a second volume about walls titled *Talking Walls: The Stories Continue*.

An event worth recognizing is Hiroshima Day or Peace Day, celebrated on August 6, the anniversary of the bombing of Japan that ended World War II. The effects of radiation from the atomic bomb affected many people as described in *Sadako*, written by Eleanor Coerr and illustrated by Ed Young. This is the true story of a young Japanese girl who tried to ward off death by following the Japanese tradition of making a thousand paper cranes. A statue of Sadako stands today in Hiroshima Peace Park. Students could learn to make origami cranes as they remember Sadako and others who died in the bombing. This is another book to use in studying the theme of war and conflict.

Another book to share connected with the theme of war was first published in 1951. *Faithful Elephants: A True Story of Animals, People, and War* by Yukio Tsuchiya is a touching story of a zoo staff's attempts to save their beloved elephants when bombs fell on Japan. People were worried about dangerous animals that might escape from the zoo, so the army ordered that all animals be killed. The trainer had to watch his trusting elephants grow weaker and weaker until they died. The three faithful elephants are buried in a tomb on the zoo grounds in Tokyo. Illustrated with water color paintings by Ted Lewin, this story, which is difficult to read aloud, tells us about the effects of war beyond guns and bombs.

The accomplishments of noted explorers are often presented in informational picture books. A number of authors have written about the ship *Endurance*, which was caught in the ice of Antarctica in 1914. Elizabeth Kimmel tells this story in *Ice Story: Shackleton's Lost Expedition* with photographs by Frank Hurley. Although he never crossed the continent or reached the South Pole, this explorer's story is remarkable. Read portions of this book aloud to introduce a theme study on leadership and courage.

Cutaway Train, written by Jon Richards and illustrated by Simon Tegg and Ross Walton, is a fascinating history of the railroad and its contribution to early U.S. history. Handsome paintings plus photographs inform the reader about the great variety of trains in the world and the kind of work they do. A number of cutaways show the inner workings of specific trains. This book could serve as a beginning to a study of transportation or the railroad in U.S. history.

World Religions

The world religions are frequently mentioned in daily newspapers, but many of us have little understanding of the basic tenets of these religions. Middle school students could undertake a theme study called "Beliefs of Peoples Around the World." Or, a group could focus on the Bible as literature. Following are some picture books that might introduce one of these studies.

Patricia and Fredrick McKissack wrote a fine book about the Bible, illustrated by James E. Ransome. *Let My People Go: Bible Stories Told by a Freeman of Color* contains 12 stories from the Bible. Each is introduced by the fictional characters Charlotte Jeffries and her father, Price, who relate the stories to the lives of African Americans as well as to the Jews and other oppressed peoples.

Jane Yolen authored a beautiful book, *O Jerusalem*, illustrated by John Thompson. This ancient city, which is a holy place for Jews, Muslims, and Christians, is often in the news as the people try to work out peaceful relations. This book leads students to the map of the Near East and the setting for the Biblical tales. It could also lend interest to the discussion of current events. Students can research information about current peace struggles on the Internet and in the library.

There are some fine picture books about different religions. For example, Demi wrote and illustrated a book titled *Buddha* (Holt, 1996). Students might compare Demi's book with that of the same title by Susan L. Roth. Both tell of Siddhartha who became Buddha, founder of a great religion. Illustrations in both books are outstanding. Roth uses brightly colored collages composed largely of handmade paper. See also *Sikh* by Catherine Chambers and *The Story of Religion*, written by Betsy Maestro and illustrated by Giulio Maestro.

How our planet and all its life forms were created is a subject of continuing interest. Novelist Virginia Hamilton retells many of the stories from different cultures in *In the Beginning: Creation Stories from Around the World*, illustrated by Barry Moser. This book won the Newbery Honor Book Award. Creation stories provide excellent material for developing a Readers Theatre presentation. This topic also would be an exciting class study using such books as those suggested below.

Julius Lester, who has written many fine books for children, authored a collection of unique creation stories, *When the Beginning Began*, illustrated by Emily Lisker. He also wrote a humorous creation tale, *What a Truly Cool World*, based on a traditional African American folk tale, illustrated by Joe Cepeda. You can learn more about this African American and his way of thinking by reading the article he wrote, "Writing About Religion," in *Book Links*.

Additional creation tales include the following:

At Break of Day, written by Nikki Grimes and illustrated by Paul Morin.

Noah's Ark by Peter Spier. This text consists only of the author's translation of a 17th-century poem, "The Flood," by Jacobus Revius. Presented on one page at the beginning of the book, the poem spells out the full story succinctly. After that, the details are supplied by Spier's amazing illustrations, which won the Caldecott Award. In some sense, this is a wordless book, because the reader must retell the story of Noah and the animals who enter the ark as pictured by Spiers.

Holidays

Picture books can be very useful in introducing discussions about the holidays we celebrate. Here is a sampling of the kinds of books available.

The winter holidays may suggest discussions about Christmas and Hanukkah. Michael J. Rosen's appealing story *Elijah's Angel*, illustrated by Aminah Brenda Lynn Robinson, demonstrates how people of different faiths can celebrate together. The art of woodcarving is featured. (Stories about Hanukkah are mentioned in Chapter 6 also.)

Interracial and intergenerational themes also can be included in discussions about holidays. In Mary Hoffman's *An Angel Just Like Me*, illustrated by Cornelius Van Wright and Ying-Hwa Hu, an African American family searches for a Christmas angel that looks like them. See also the Venn Diagram Lesson on comparing two versions of the story of Las Posadas on page 118.

Thanksgiving is a theme and a holiday that inspires the study of U.S. history and consideration of what we are thankful for. Many picture books present these concepts; for instance, Eve Bunting's *Dreaming of America: An Ellis Island Story*, illustrated by Ben F. Stahl. Bunting combines the theme of immigration with giving thanks. Another attractive picture book is *Molly's Pilgrim*, which questions the assumption that everyone knows the definition of a Pilgrim. Written by Barbara

Cohen and illustrated by Daniel Mark Duffy, in this tale a Russian Jewish woman helps her daughter dress her doll as a Pilgrim who looks exactly like herself, and a teacher helps children realize the full meaning of the word *pilgrim*.

Halloween is another holiday with an interesting history. *Day of the Dead* by Diane Hoyt-Goldsmith with photographs by Lawrence Migdale shows how a Latino family in California celebrates this holiday. A funny book that reveals a different perspective of Halloween is Erica Silverman's *The Halloween House*, illustrated by Jon Agee. Basing her text on an old verse, Silverman recounts a story about vampires, cats, and witches who live in a haunted house. At the same time the illustrator tells another story about two escaped convicts who, after spending the night in this house, are happy to return to their "Home Sweet Home," a jail cell.

Discovering Information About Science and Mathematics

Picture books have much to offer older students as they explore topics in science and mathematics. Following are the kinds of books you can find to enhance your curriculum.

Taking Care of Our Planet: A Theme Study

Taking care of our planet is a topic that frequently appears in daily newspapers. We read about efforts to save the rain forests in Brazil, to maintain the swamps in Florida, and to avoid polluting the air worldwide. Plan a theme study titled "Taking Care of Our Planet." The culminating activity for the study might be a presentation for a first- or second-grade class including a play or puppet show, songs, a mural, and a few questions to talk about with these children. Introduce this study by bringing in various picture books as described in the following pages. (This section has been adapted from Tiedt, I. 1999.)

Introducing stewardship. You might begin the study by reading aloud the charming narrative *Stuartship*, written by Ryan Collay and Joanne Dubrow and illustrated by Sydney Roark. (See the illustration on page 4.) The title is a play on words, as the main character is Stuart who learns about stewardship from a wise elder. The story centers on Stuart's fear that his neighbor, Mr. Goodwin, is going to cut down an old apple tree that Stuart considers his own. See Appendix A,

Thinking + Lesson Plan 1 (see page 142), for a lesson plan based on this book, referred to in Chapter 1.

Read this narrative aloud, showing students the illustrations as you go. (Have multiple copies available so students can examine the detailed drawings as you read.) Pause to discuss the questions that the authors have inserted throughout the book. Following the reading, write this question on the chalkboard: What did Stuart learn about stewardship? Have each student write a paragraph in reply. Students can share this writing in small groups before beginning an investigation of a group of books about the topic assigned to them.

The Magic School Bus series often focuses on topics relating to conservation, for example, *The Magic School Bus in the Rain Forest*, written by Joanna Cole and illustrated by Bruce Degen. This highly illustrated narrative relates the story of Ms. Frizzle and her class as they travel to the tropics to investigate the rainforest. This kind of book can serve as a model for students who are making reports or planning an original children's book. The text is an engaging mix of narrative and factual data.

Andrew Glass tells an amusing tale about Johnny Appleseed and his brother, Nathaniel, in *Folks Call Me Appleseed John*, a story mentioned in Chapter 3. This is only one story about John Chapman, the man who traveled across the wilderness planting apple seeds to create apple orchards. Not everyone realizes that Chapman was an early conservationist. The oil paintings in this picture book are outstanding.

Earth Keepers by Joan Anderson explains the importance of taking care of our planet through a photo essay format. Black-and-white photographs by George Ancona depict three conservation efforts set in different locations in the United States. This book leads children to think about how they can be Earth keepers, too. It would be excellent motivation for a media production as students produce a photo essay based on local efforts to care for our planet.

Jean Craighead George, noted naturalist and author, presents a story with a lesson in *Everglades*. Five children accompanied by a storyteller guide explore this fascinating environment. Paintings by Wendell Minor enhance and further explain the text. The author encourages readers to consider how they can help protect the environment.

Ecology. Ecology, too, is the focus of some attractive picture books for young people. Janice VanCleave's *Ecology for Every Kid: Easy Activities that Make Learning Science Fun* engages readers in experiments that involve conservation. The author introduces the topics of ecology and conservation and provides general directions for conducting the activities in this book, which is part of an extensive series of science books by VanCleave. Activities focus on topics such as acid rain, the food chain, adapting to environments, and different biomes. Another resource book is Michael Scott's *The Young Oxford Book of Ecology*. The author begins with a discussion of ecology and why it matters. Following the presentation of extensive information about animals and the major biomes, he includes a 12-page section titled "Threats to Life" that addresses human impact on the Earth and how we can leave the planet fit for the future.

Endangered animals. Another aspect of conservation that is intriguing to young people is the extinct animal, for example, the auk and the dodo, and the importance of taking care of wildlife. Endangered species have received attention in the news as environmentalists plead for saving the habitats necessary to animals such as the spotted owl and the manatee.

Macmillan has published a complete *Guide to Endangered Animals* by Roger Few. Following a well-written introduction that extols the wonderful diversity of life on Earth, the author categorizes endangered animals by continent. Here, too, is a clear summary of the problems that wildlife face, namely, the destruction of natural habits, pollution, and killing by humans in various ways. Included also is a brief discussion of the controversies that arise in making decisions relating to conservation, for example, the plight of the great bustard, which is being pushed from its native grasslands by increased farming in central Asia. Excellent photographs and drawings from varied sources make this a useful book for all ages.

A Cincinnati Zoo book, *Saving Endangered Birds: Ensuring a Future in the Wild* by Thane Maynard, focuses on bird life. Maps help the reader locate the habitats of the birds around the world. Full-page photographs show each bird in a natural setting. Birds such as the Micronesian kingfisher and the exotic quetzal, which lives in Central America and southern Mexico, are featured. A page of information about each bird describes its appearance, range, and feeding habits. Important to the concern for conservation are the comments about threats to the bird and specific efforts such as laws, organizations, and refuges to protect the birds.

A different perspective is provided in *Vanishing Habitats* by Noel Simon. The author explains what a habitat is and discusses the various kinds of habitats, for example, rain forests, deserts, and tundra. He explains problems relating to population growth, mining, erosion, and use of the ocean as a dumping place for poisonous waste. Although presented in picture book format, this book provides an excellent overview for older students of the need to maintain the delicate balance between human progress and nature so that we do not destroy our wildlife.

Appreciating nature. Many books about plants and animals help develop positive attitudes toward conservation. Middle school students could share some of these books with younger children to help them learn about the importance of taking care of our planet.

A beautiful picture book, *Loon Lake* by Ron Hirschi, invites the reader to "Paddle with me quietly, slowly." The author guides us to observe the great blue heron, frogs, and waterlilies—life along a waterway near a small lake. This would be a wonderful book to share before or after taking students on a field trip through a refuge where such wildlife abounds. Superb photographs by Daniel J. Cox add to the beauty of this book, which focuses on a pair of loons who come to nest on the lake. Anyone who has heard the haunting song of the loon will enjoy sharing this poetic book. An afterword provides more information about loons and a source for obtaining materials featuring loon protection efforts. Older students could use this book as a model for creating original books for children.

A factual presentation, *Marshes & Swamps* by Gail Gibbons, tells us how wetlands are formed. The text presented in large type explains the evolution from a marsh to a swamp and where these kinds of land forms are located. Detailed illustrations depict the various kinds of plants and animals that live in the swamp. The author differentiates between freshwater and saltwater swamps and gives the wildlife characteristic in each. Especially interesting are the mangrove swamps in Florida. Described as "some of the most unusual landscapes in the world," swamps are full of surprises. Students who enjoy informational books might use this book as a model for creating a picture text.

The Sierra Club, an organization known for its efforts to protect the environment, publishes a series of books for children about the Earth and its creatures. One example is *Do Not Disturb: The Mysteries of Animal Hibernation and Sleep* by Margery Facklam. Realistic black-and-white drawings of the animals that hibernate are the work of Pamela Johnson. The factual text describes the habits of these animals beginning with the grizzly bear, which sleeps all winter. The author also presents animals that are dormant for shorter periods of time, for example, bats and possums. In addition, there is an interesting discussion of sleep, the circadian rhythm that animals follow, and why we, and other animals, dream.

After students investigate the picture books assigned to their group, they should summarize what they have learned, reporting to the class. The class can then plan ways to share this information with primary grade children.

Scientists and Scientific Discoveries

Picture books are wonderful resources from which students can learn about science and scientists. A short presentation of one of these books by the teacher may stimulate further study by an individual or a cooperative learning group. The books also provide models for student reports, giving them ideas about making their writing more interesting, a topic worth discussing with the class.

A beautiful biography about Galileo Galilei was created by talented artist and writer Peter Sis. *Starry Messenger: A Book Depicting the Life of a Famous Scientist, Mathematician, Astronomer, Philosopher, and Physicist, Galileo Galilei* features a succinct text in large print. Sis's full-page illustrations further explicate the work of this man who made major contributions to the world of knowledge.

Pat and Linda Cummings present information about 12 contemporary scientists in *Talking with Adventurers: Conversations with Christina M. Allen, Robert Ballard, Michael L. Blakey, Ann Bowles, David Doubilet, Jane Goodall, Dereck and Beverly Joubert, Michael Novacek, Johan Reinhard, Rick C. West, and Juris Zarins*. Each short presentation in interview format could be read aloud and discussed. The format used suggests a different way of reporting information about persons students are investigating. The author includes maps on which to locate the fieldwork of each scientist, plus a glossary. She also lists Internet sites for further exploration. The book, published by the National Geographic Society, would be an excellent resource for both science and language arts teachers.

In a different approach to science Debra Frasier combines fiction and fact as she explores the beach in *Out of the Ocean*. Her art includes full-color photographs and intriguing collages to share the treasures that wash up on the shore. This book would be an excellent introduction to a day at the beach. It also could serve as a model for writing a report of findings based on observation or research.

Make the study of the human body more exciting by sharing the oversized picture book written by Richard Platt and illustrated by the well-known artist Stephen Biesty. The book, titled *Stephen Biesty's Incredible Body*, begins with these amazing words:

> Extraordinary Exploration Squad reporting for duty! Our mission: to explore and map every corner of an unknown territory—the human body. The chosen subject: Stephen Biesty; gender—male; profession—artist.

So, the story continues with a journey through Biesty's body illustrated in colorful detail and explained with numerous asides and cross-sections for which this artist is famous. This author/illustrator team have worked together to produce such other titles as *Steve Biesty's Incredible Cross-Sections, Steve Biesty's Cross-Sections Castle, Steve Biesty's Cross-Section Man-of-War, Steve Biesty's Incredible Explosions*, and *Steve Biesty's Incredible Everything*. All are well worth your examination.

Dinosaurs hold special intrigue for students of all ages. One of the picture books that presents these creatures in great detail is *I Didn't Know That Dinosaurs Laid Eggs*, written by Kate Petty and illustrated by a team of artists and designers headed by Robert Perry. Although only 32 pages long, this informative picture book includes a glossary and an index.

A very unusual illustrated book about dinosaurs is the wordless presentation *Time Flies* by Eric Rothmann. A bird flies into a natural history museum where it passes the numerous exhibits that seem to come alive. Students can identify the dinosaurs and flying reptiles depicted in Rothmann's oil paintings. Add to the fun of a study with middle schoolers by sharing dinosaur riddles such as the following, written by Noelle Sterne and illustrated by Victoria Chess, in *Tyrannosaurus Wrecks: A Book of Dinosaur Riddles*:

What did the mother dinosaur say when she saw her child's room? ("What a mess-ozoic!")

How did things begin? That's something that always interests students. They will especially enjoy *Peanuts, Popcorn, Ice Cream, Candy, and Soda Pop and How They Began* by Solveig P. Russell. Illustrated by Ralph McDonald, this book demonstrates how interesting research can be. Students may be motivated to explore favorite topics in the library and on the Internet.

Space and Space Travel

The study of space and space travel has special intrigue today as technology becomes more advanced. Following are a few picture books that could serve as models for students who plan to create children's books (see also Chapter 8).

David Kirk's *Nova's Ark*, illustrated with bold futuristic paintings, tells the story of Nova, a boy who has a tiny bedroom high above the city of Roton. He treasures a set of wooden animals and an ark made in the early days of Roton, passed on to him by his father. Nova's class takes a fieldtrip to the space center and sits at the console of a real Glax Cruiser, and the teacher tells Nova, "That's the place for you…. Someday you'll fly into space like your father. Exploration is in your wiring!" And Nova does fly into space accidentally for a wonderful adventure. This book will intrigue students interested in robots and the way they work.

Middle school students are exposed to many videotapes and movies set in space. How many students have seen *Star Wars*? Many students will enjoy the marvelous illustrations and detailed information presented in *Star Wars Episode I: The*

Visual Dictionary, written by David West Reynolds and expanded with photographs and other art by a team managed by Cathy Tincknell. This oversized picture book is based on the film and may motivate students to read it to clarify the fictional setting, information about characters, and factual details about how things work. Presented as a visual dictionary, this book was never meant for primary grade children, but it's perfect for middle schoolers.

The Best Book of Spaceships, written by Ian and Aan Graham and illustrated by a team headed by Ch'en-Ling, also presents fascinating nonfiction about spacecraft. Detailed illustrations help explain the text and a glossary and index support the presentation.

Focus on Math

Math concepts do not appear as frequently in picture books as do other ideas. However, there are some books worth noting that may enhance math instruction or assist students for whom math is difficult.

Older students will enjoy reviewing counting books that they can use with young children or as models for books they can create. There are many of these types to choose from, for example, *Brian Wildsmith's 1,2,3's* with its flamboyant art, or *Count!* by Denise Fleming. Miriam Schlein with illustrator Donald Crews picture things that are *More Than One*. Students will enjoy listing all kinds of grouped "ones," such as one week, one flock, one year, one herd, and so on.

Dealing with larger numbers into the millions can prove tricky. Dr. Seuss plays with numbers in *The 500 Hats of Bartholomew Cubbins*. In this story a little boy cannot take off his hat to honor the king because another hat keeps appearing. Mathematician David Schwartz wrote *How Much Is a Million?*, illustrated by Stephen Kellogg. Later he wrote *G Is for Googol*, illustrated by Marissa Moss. This alphabet book deals with math concepts with clarity but good humor. Schwartz also wrote *On Beyond a Million*, illustrated by Paul Meisel, in which he uses popcorn to illustrate number concepts.

Students who have difficulty with math might find books that deal with such processes as multiplication helpful. In *Anno's Mysterious Multiplying Jar*, Masaichiro and Mitsumasa Anno begin with 1 island and work up to 10 jars. Then they progress to larger numbers.

A clever story from India is presented by Demi, titled *One Grain of Rice: A Mathematical Folktale*. Her wonderfully detailed paintings include two impressive double-page spreads. Demi tells the tale of the rice the clever Rani requested as a reward from the unsuspecting rajah—one grain of rice doubled each day for 30 days!

Students can follow the summary chart showing that Rani received more than one billion grains of rice, enough to feed all the hungry people during a famine.

Estimating is a skill that can be introduced through picture books such as Rod Clement's *Counting on Frank*, in which funny illustrations engage readers in mathematical operations. Stuart J. Murphy wrote *Betcha!*, illustrated by S.D. Schindler, which centers on guessing how many jelly beans are in a jar, then leads to other interesting estimates. The author includes other activities you can introduce with this book.

Dealing with money is another mathematical concept presented in picture book format. David Schwartz created a book about money titled, *If You Made a Million*, illustrated delightfully by Steven Kellogg. He discusses what happens to the money we put in banks, how checking accounts work, and so on.

A math professor, Julie Glass, became so excited about involving students with mathematics that she decided to write books for young people. She first wrote *The Fly on the Ceiling: A Math Myth*, which tells about the famous French philosopher and mathematican Rene Descartes. Her second book, *A Dollar for Penny*, tells about a young female entrepreneur who has a lemonade stand and saves her money.

Remember, too, that such mathematical processes as probability theory (in the form of prediction) can be presented with any reading lesson. Encourage students to predict what a story will be about just from reading the title. They also can predict what will happen next or how a story will end. Students can use graphs to present information about a story, and they can use a Venn diagram to formulate comparisons. Thus, while using mathematical skills, they are exercising their thinking abilities and they are learning concepts.

Studying Folklore Across the Curriculum

Folklore is a unifying theme that appears around the world. Found in the literature of every country and every ethnic group, folklore is linked closely to storytelling because the tales were passed orally from generation to generation. Although it began orally, folklore more recently has been recorded on tape, in print, and on film.

A study of folklore easily can be related to history and geography units as well as the language arts curriculum, and an integrated humanities approach is particularly well suited for the study of folklore. Moreover, a study of folklore includes a wide range of different cultures, thus giving students insight into how much we are alike as we teach through the use of story. Folk tales are particularly appropriate for enriching social studies and literature studies as students dramatize, retell, or discover several versions of these popular tales. Folklore even enhances the study of science and mathematics, thus it crosses the total curriculum.

The best presentations of folk tales are found in beautifully illustrated picture books housed in the children's book section of the library. However, the stories are not necessarily suitable for children in the early elementary grades, but may be more appropriate for older children in upper elementary and middle school years. Following is a selection of just a few of the many folk tales in children's literature.

Folklore Around the World

A fine collection of folk tales from different countries is *Tales Alive: Ten Multicultural Folktales with Activities*. The tales are retold by Susan Milord and illustrated with paintings by Michael A. Donato. Tales included come from Russia, Argentina, India, Ghana, Canada, Scotland, Italy, Australia, Japan, and Turkey. A variety of learning activities are suggested following each story.

The texture of life and the colors of Cameroon are interwoven in *The Fortune Tellers* (Dutton, 1992), a tale of a young man who wants to see what his future holds. Written by Lloyd Alexander and illustrated by Trina Schart Hyman, this is a good story for acting out.

Julia Gukova tells the story of *The Mole's Daughter*. This Korean story features the humble mole's attempt to connect with the power of the sun, clouds, wind, and so forth.

Written by David Kherdian and illustrated by Nonny Hogrogian, *The Golden Bracelet* follows a familiar pattern. This old Armenian tale tells of a young prince, Haig, and the beautiful peasant girl, Anahid, who would only marry a man who was master of a craft.

Lore from Germany must certainly include the work of the two Grimm brothers, whose collection of fairy tales has made a lasting contribution to world literature. Many of their tales appear in picture book format including the familiar story *Seven at a Blow: A Tale from the Brothers Grimm*, retold by Eric A. Kimmel and illustrated by Megan Lloyd. Another example is a less known tale, *Ouch! A Tale from Grimm*, retold by Natalie Babbitt and illustrated by Fred Marcellino.

Lore from France, similarly, must include the beautiful fairy tales by Charles Perrault: *Sleeping Beauty, Cinderella, Little Red Riding Hood*, and others. See the lovely collection illustrated by Janusz Grabianski, *Perrault's Classic French Fairy Tales*. Another collection, illustrated by Michael Hague, is *Cinderella and Other Tales from Perrault*.

The tale of *The Donkey and the Rock*, retold and illustrated by Demi, can be traced to the years before Christ. Originating in India, the story tells of two merchants traveling to market with their loaded donkeys. The donkey owned by one man breaks the oil jar of the other man on a rock. They ask the king for help in determining justice. Because he could not see that either man was at fault, the king arrested the donkey and the rock. This would be a wonderful story to act out. The beautiful watercolors suggest art techniques for students to emulate, too.

Authors often take liberties in retelling folk tales that have originated in the oral tradition. Janice del Negro creates her own distinctive version of a Celtic folktale in *Lucy Dove*, illustrated eerily by Leonid Gore. This spooky tale features a strong female, Lucy, who is not afraid of the boggle that comes forth from a grave where she sits sewing.

Written by Francine Prose and illustrated by Mark Podwal, *You Never Know: A Legend of the Lamed-Vavniks* tells how a humble shoemaker saved the town of Plotchnik, which had had no rain for 40 days. According to Jewish tradition, lamed-vavniks are holy people who live humbly and anonymously in every community.

Skillful storyteller Robert D. San Souci and illustrator Brian Pinkney combine talents to present *The Faithful Friend*. This West Indian folk tale tells the story of courage and true friendship of Clement and Hippolyte, two men who live on the Caribbean island of Martinique. The author includes a glossary of West Indian words. The book would fit well with the theme study of friendship described earlier.

A study of Russia should include the lore about the witch Baba Yaga. This wicked witch appears in many folk tales. Sometimes she is kind and helpful, but more often she is mean and known to eat her children (by mistake, of course). She lives in the dark woods in a tiny cottage that has "chicken legs" and can turn around at her command. (See the illustration on page 92.) She flies round the world in a giant mortar and pestle. This is a great story to act out. One of the best presentations of the story is *Babayaga*, written by Ernest Small and illustrated by Blair Lent (Ernest Small is a pseudonym used by the well-known illustrator Blair Lent, so this popular book was both written and illustrated by Blair Lent.) Another version of this tale with the same title is retold and illustrated by Katya Arnold, who was born in Moscow. *The Gigantic Turnip*, retold by Aleksei Tolstoy and illustrated with humorous detail by Niamh Sharkey, is another traditional Russian story that is good for an oral storytelling presentation.

A rich source of folklore is derived from Native American cultures. For example, the story *Snail Girl Brings Water: A Navajo Story*, told by Geri Keams and illustrated by Richard Ziehler-Martin, comes from Arizona where water is scarce. This pourquoi tale explains why the snail carries moisture on its back and leaves a trail wherever it goes. One of the best known authors and illustrators who specializes in Native American lore is Paul Goble. He has a whole series of books about the Plains Indian trickster, Iktomi, for example, *Iktomi Loses His Eyes*. Goble inserts all kinds of whimsical touches in this book; for example, he writes in the Dedication: "This book is for Iktomi's friends—this means you." Paul Goble is also well known for other tales such as *Beyond the Ridge*, which tells of the Indian's way of handling death. If you plan a unit of study that involves Native American cultures, be sure to locate Paul Goble's work; he has about 30 titles in print, and they are all well regarded by Native American leaders.

A study of folklore easily can be integrated into the social studies as students become more familiar with the peoples of the world. It connects readily, too, with map study. Read a few tales aloud to students as you locate the setting for each story on the map. Then provide a selection of folk tales from different countries. Have students work in groups as they read the story and decide how to present the tale to other members of their class. These presentations might be shared in an assembly for other classes or the Parent Teacher Association.

Comparing Different Versions of One Tale

Cinderella is a natural choice for comparing because there is a Cinderella story in the folklore of almost every country. Begin with the original version by Charles Perrault, perhaps as retold by Amy Ehrlich. Let students compare some of the following versions plus any others your librarian may suggest:

Ieh-Shen: A Cinderella Story from China, written by Ai-Ling Louie and illustrated by Ed Young

Cinderella: Or the Little Glass Slipper by Marcia Brown (Caldecott Award winner)

The Egyptian Cinderella, written by Shirley Climo and illustrated by Ruth Heller

The Korean Cinderella, written by Shirley Climo and illustrated by Ruth Heller

The Persian Cinderella, written by Shirley Climo and illustrated by Robert Florczak

Angkat, the Cambodian Cinderella, written by Jewell R. Coburn and illustrated by Eddie Flotte

Jouanah: A Hmong Cinderella, written by Jewell R. Coburn with Tzexa Cherta Lee and illustrated by Anne Sibley O'Brien

Cinderella, retold by Amy Ehrlich and illustrated by Susan Jeffers

The Golden Sandal: A Middle Eastern Cinderella Story, written by Rebecca Hickox and illustrated by Will Hillenbrand (This tale is based on Iraqui lore.)

The Way Meat Loves Salt: A Cinderella Tale from the Jewish Tradition, written by Nina Jaffe and illustrated by Louise August

Cendrillon: A Caribbean Cinderella, written by Robert D. San Souci and illustrated by Brian Pinkney (This version contains French Creole words and phrases and African American characters.)

Sootface: An Ojibwa Cinderella Story, retold by Robert D. San Souci and illustrated by Brian Pinkney

Raisel's Riddle, written by Erica Silverman and illustrated by Susan Gaber (This version features a Jewish Cinderella who poses a clever riddle to challenge the rabbi's son.)

Mufaro's Beautiful Daughters by John Steptoe (Caldecott Award winner)

Have students note the variations in the various versions of *Cinderella*. For example, in the Ojibwa version, only the woman who could see the handsome, but invisible warrior, would be his bride. Although her sisters tried first, it was Sootface who saw her future husband. Use a Venn diagram to guide students in comparing versions of Cinderella, as shown in Venn Diagram Lesson: Comparing Versions of Cinderella worksheet on the following page.

There are more versions of *Cinderella* than there are of any other tale. However, you will find enough versions of other tales so that students can make comparative studies of those as well. For example, look for different versions of *Stone Soup*. One version is written by Heather Forest and illustrated by Susan Gaber. See how many different versions of this old tale students can find. Perhaps the most famous is that illustrated by Marcia Brown, originally published by Scribner in 1947. In the Swedish version, the soup begins with a nail. In the Russian version it begins with an axe. In all versions, however, the end is the same: The villagers share what they have created cooperatively. Some classes might also have fun cooking "stone soup."

Look also for the following popular tales. Have students search for different versions of each one. This is a terrific activity for gifted students.

Seven at a Blow: A Tale from the Brothers Grimm, retold by Eric Kimmel and illustrated by Megan Lloyd

The Pied Piper of Hamelin, written by Robert Holden and illustrated by Drahos Zak (This tale would be great for acting out.)

Any version of the fairy tale *Rumplestiltskin* plus *Rumplestiltskin's Daughter* by Diane Stanley, which continues the original story.

Conclusion

In Chapter 7 we have examined picture books that can be used to support learning across the curriculum. I suggested books that introduce geography and

Venn Diagram Lesson: Compare Versions of *Cinderella*

Directions

In this exercise you will compare different versions of the story *Cinderella*.

Read each book, then write adjectives in each circle that describe that version of the story. In the overlapping section, write adjectives that describe both versions being compared.

1. First, compare *Mufaro's Beautiful Daughters* and *The Egyptian Cinderella*.

2. Then, compare *The Egyptian Cinderella* and the more familiar *Cinderella: Or the Little Glass Slipper*.

3. Finally, review your findings and decide on several conclusions you can write at the bottom of this sheet. For example, what was present in all versions? What were several unique features that appeared in only one version?

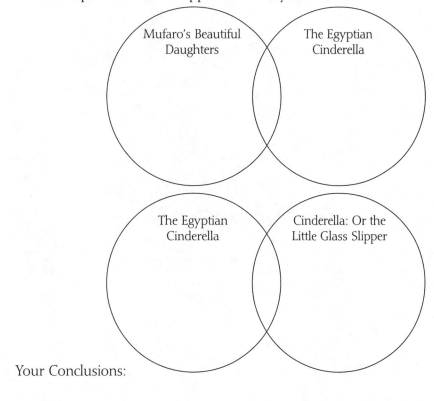

Your Conclusions:

Venn Diagram Lesson. *Teaching With Picture Books in the Middle School* by Iris McClellan Tiedt, ©2000 International Reading Association. May be copied.

history topics as well as those that can be used to support the science and math curricula. In a final section I addressed the study of folklore that crosses the entire curriculum. This section concluded with a comparative study of the familiar folk tale *Cinderella*. In Chapter 8 we will continue working across the curriculum as we explore picture books that stimulate creativity related to art and music.

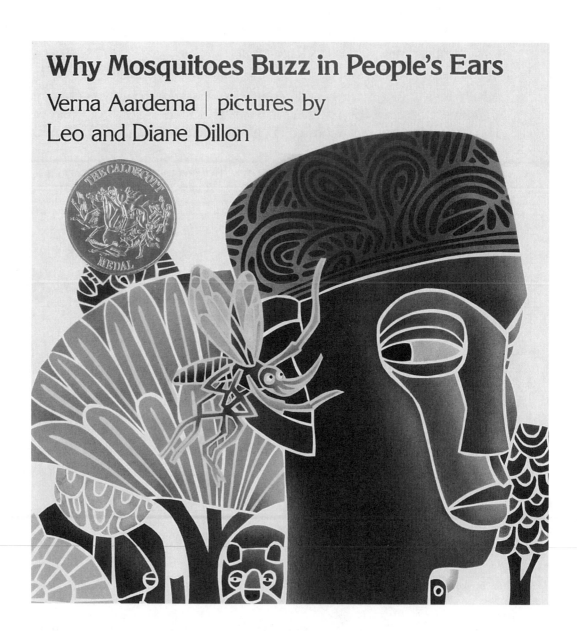

Why Mosquitoes Buzz in People's Ears

Verna Aardema | pictures by
Leo and Diane Dillon

Stimulating Creativity

Middle school students will enjoy participating in creative activities that lend interest and variety to their studies. Reluctant readers, for example, may read as they are engaged in producing art, something for which they show talent. Others may respond to opportunities to engage in music—singing, composing music, or choreographing dance routines. Picture books have much to offer as a stimulus for art and music.

Appreciating the Art in Picture Books

Bring to your classroom a collection of picture books that students can examine with particular emphasis on the art of the illustrator. Have students work in pairs as they look at the art in two different books. Include books illustrated by such noted artists as these (Note that when no illustrator is named, the book has been written and illustrated by one person.):

Why Mosquitoes Buzz in People's Ears, written by Verna Aardema and illustrated by Leo and Diane Dillon (Caldecott Award winner; see the illustration on the facing page.)

The Desert Is Theirs, written by Byrd Baylor and illustrated by Peter Parnell (Caldecott Honor Book)

The Donkey and the Rock by Demi

Drummer Hoff, written by Barbara Emberley and illustrated by Ed Emberley

Out of the Ocean by Debra Frasier

In Joseph's Yard by Charles Keeping

The Beastly Feast, written by Bruce Goldstone and illustrated by Blair Lent

The Boy Who Held Back the Sea by Thomas Locker

Arrow to the Sun: A Pueblo Indian Tale by Gerald McDermott

Sam, Bangs & Moonshine by Evaline Ness (Caldecott Honor Book)

Mola: Cuna Life, Stories and Art by Maricel E. Presilla

Shaker Lane by Alice and Martin Provensen

Jewels, written by Belinda Rochelle and illustrated by Cornelius Van Wright and Ying-Hwa Hu

Cendrillon: A Caribbean Cinderella, written by Robert San Souci and illustrated by Brian Pinkney

May I Bring a Friend?, written by Beatrice Schenk de Regniers and illustrated by Beni Montresor

Snow by Uri Shulevitz (Caldecott Honor Book)

Stevie by John Steptoe

This is just a sampling of the wonderfully illustrated books that you might choose. Refer to the list of Caldecott Award winners in Appendix B. Also ask your librarian to suggest others as you develop Thinking + Lesson Plan 12, Evaluating the Art in Picture Books, in Appendix A (see page 153).

Identifying Various Artistic Media

As you select books for Thinking + Lesson Plan 12, choose those that demonstrate different kinds of art techniques using varied media. Also, make a point of including the work of noted illustrators, in addition to those in the earlier list, whose work appears in many picture books, for example: Marcia Brown, Barbara Cooney, Tom Feelings, Paul Galdone, Ezra Jack Keats, Susan Jeffries, Leo Lionni, Arnold Lobel, Robert McCloskey, Jerry Pinkney, Brian Wildsmith, Jeanette Winter, and Ed Young.

This lesson would be especially fitting during the weeks before you plan to have students create original picture books as described later in this chapter. In addition to the many books already described throughout this text, several specific books that feature various artistic media are as follows:

No Mirrors in My Nana's House, written by Ysaye M. Barnwell and illustrated by Synthia Saint James. The paintings by Saint James are done in rich primary colors showing human figures in stylized form. Her painting looks much like cut paper work, which some students might find appealing. This book also includes a CD-ROM on which the author's words are sung by the group Sweet Honey in the Rock.

Baby High, Baby Low, written by Stella Blackstone and illustrated by Denise and Fernando. This illustrator uses bold fabric designs and stylized human figures.

Out of the Ocean by Debra Frasier. Creator of the beautiful book *On the Day That You Were Born,* Frasier uses mixed media effectively. Here she combines photographs and bold paintings to create striking collages that complement the words of the story.

On the Wings of Eagles: An Ethiopian Boy's Story by Jeffery Schrier. This author/illustrator presents outstanding art in this picture book. He uses collage and fuses diverse materials electronically, bringing together documentary photographs, ancient crafts, and line drawings placed on a background of an original Ethiopian robe.

Dear Mili by Maurice Sendak. This is an especially fine example of Sendak's art. The book is based on a previously undiscovered story by Wilhelm Grimm, which was found in a letter that Grimm wrote to a young girl in 1816. Maurice Sendak is perhaps best known for *Where the Wild Things Are,* which won the Caldecott Award. As Sendak wrote in *Contemporary Authors,* "I am trying to draw the way children feel—or rather the way I know I felt as a child."

Experimenting With Art Techniques

Students usually enjoy art activities and the change of pace from more common reading and writing activities. In the art activity described in Thinking + Lesson Plan 13 in Appendix A (see page 154), for example, students will produce paper that may be used for the cover of a project report or for the background on which original poetry can be displayed. In this lesson the paper is used to share appreciation for the diverse population in the United States.

Introducing Selected Artists

Often we forget to identify the artist who created the illustrations in an outstanding picture book. Students should get to know these artists and the kind of art they produce. Be sure to include artists who represent different racial and ethnic groups.

Introduce students to talented female artist Faith Ringgold, who creates impressive large story quilts that hang on museum walls usually seen only by adults.

You can examine her pictured stories from a distance to see the whole picture or view them up close to observe the textures she uses. She is the subject of an excellent picture book biography titled *Faith Ringgold* by Robyn Montana Turner, which is part of the series Portraits of Women Artists for Children. Many of Ringgold's works appear in this biography. You might reproduce the following quotation from this book to display while focusing on this artist's work:

> After I decided to be an artist, the first thing that I had
> to believe was that I, a black woman, could be on the art scene
> without sacrificing one iota of my blackness, or my femaleness,
> or my humanity.
>
> Faith Ringgold

Young people became familiar with Ringgold's exceptional art when one of her story quilts was developed into a picture book, *Tar Beach*, which tells about life in Harlem, New York, where the artist was born. Later, Ringgold wrote and illustrated a second book featuring the same characters, Cassie Louise Lightfoot and her brother. This book, *Aunt Harriet's Underground Railroad in the Sky*, tells the story of a real African American heroine, Harriet Tubman, who helped free many slaves. Ringgold combines fact and fancy in this imaginative story.

Another fine writer and artist whose work is featured in the Thinking + Lesson Plan 13 is Ezra Jack Keats. This Jewish man, whose original name was Katz, died in 1983. He is the subject of *Ezra Jack Keats: A Biography with Illustrations* by Dean Engel and Florence B. Freedman. In illustrating books written by other authors, he noticed that the main characters were never black. He said, "So I resolved that, when I had the confidence to do my own work, my hero would be a black child." In 1961 he began working on his first story about Peter, a young African American boy patterned after the photograph of a child he had clipped from the newspaper. This book, *The Snowy Day*, won the Caldecott Award that year. Delighted with the character he had created, Keats produced 19 other stories about Peter and his friends, for example, *Whistle for Willie* and *Peter's Chair*.

Another fine African American artist is Jacob Lawrence, whose paintings record the story of African Americans from the days of slavery through their gradual, but steady, migration to the northern United States. His work is presented in the handsome picture book *The Great Migration*. In this book a simple straightforward text relates the history of families like his own as they migrated from the southern United States toward the northern industrialized cities during World War I. Lawrence died in June 2000.

Tomie dePaola is a favorite artist whose work appears in many picture books. Barbara Elleman has written a biography of this artist titled *Tomie dePaola: His Art and His Stories*, which includes many examples of his illustrations. Although he has written a number of books, you might look for the following titles to begin with: *Tomie dePaola's Mother Goose*, *Strega Nona*, and *Nana Upstairs & Nana Downstairs*.

Use a Venn diagram to compare dePaola's *The Night of Las Posadas* with *Las Posadas: An Hispanic Christmas Celebration* by Diane Hoyt-Goldsmith and Lawrence Migdale. See the Venn Diagram Lesson worksheet on the next page that you can duplicate for use with your students.

Obtain at least one copy of the two versions of these picture books about Las Posadas. Set up a learning center at a table where two students can work at one time, reading each book and studying the art. Students can work together to think about the qualities of the writing and of the art in the books as directed on the study guide provided with the lesson.

As students complete their study guides, have them work in cooperative learning groups to compare their conclusions. Each group can then compose a summary paragraph to share with the whole class after everyone is ready.

A number of picture book biographies present the lives of famous artists, including examples of their work. Examine some of the following:

Most people recognize the unique picture of the farmer holding a pitchfork and his wife, who gaze sternly at us from the canvas. Born on an Iowa farm in the 1800s, Grant Wood painted the life and people he knew, thus initiating a new movement in painting called Regionalism. John Duggleday writes about this artist in *Artist in Overalls: The Life of Grant Wood*. The book's afterword guides the beginning artist in imitating Wood's style.

In *My Name Is Georgia: A Portrait*, artist Jeanette Winter has written and illustrated an attractive biography of noted artist Georgia O'Keeffe. Students could use the Internet to find more examples of this artist's diverse work. Perhaps her best-known work, *The Red Poppy*, was placed on a U.S. stamp that you may still find.

Talking with Artists, a collection of interviews with artists, was compiled by Pat Cummings. Each section of the book follows the same organization. First, the artist tells his or her story in the first person, including personal anecdotes that make the biographical information more interesting. Then, each person answers the following questions:

1. Where do you get your ideas from?

2. What is a normal day like for you?

3. Where do you work?

Venn Diagram Lesson: Comparing Two Versions of "Las Posadas"

Directions

Use this Venn diagram to compare the work of the author/illustrator Tomie dePaola and the writer/artist team Diane Hoyt-Goldsmith and Lawrence Migdale as they present a story about the same holiday, Las Posadas. Consider how the story is presented as well as the art used to interpret the text.

In Space 1 write adjectives that describe the work of dePaola. In Space 2 write adjectives that describe the work in both books. In Space 3 write adjectives that describe only the work of Hoyt-Goldsmith and Migdale.

Conclusions

Study your entries. What conclusions can you make about these two books?

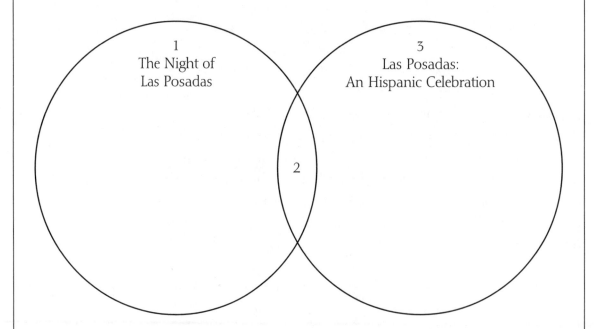

1
The Night of
Las Posadas

3
Las Posadas:
An Hispanic Celebration

2

Your Conclusions:

4. Do you have any children? Any pets?

5. What do you enjoy drawing the most?

6. Do you ever put people you know in your pictures?

7. What do you use to make your pictures?

8. How did you get to do your first book?

Artists included are Victoria Chess, Pat Cummings, Leo and Diane Dillon, Richard Egielski, Lois Ehlert, Lisa Campbell Ernst, Tom Feelings, Steven Kellogg, Jerry Pinkney, Amy Schwartz, Lane Smith, Chris Van Allsburg, and David Wiesner. Pictures of the artists both as adults and as children are included plus full color examples of their work.

Fifteen artists display their talents in a lovely edition of Martin Luther King's *I Have a Dream*. Introduced in an afterword, the artists include Leo and Diane Dillon, James Ransome, Brian Pinkney, Jerry Pinkney, Tom Feelings, and Carole Byard. Each picture illustrates a phrase from King's speech.

Creating Children's Books

Middle school students will enjoy creating original children's books. This project includes writing the content to be presented and making the illustrations that accompany the text, so the activity integrates art across the curriculum. Further, students can learn to bind their books so that they are professional in appearance. As the students complete their books, they can decide how to share them in various ways with young children and with their own families.

Although the possibilities for creating children's books are endless, in this chapter I focus on categories that place the emphasis on the art of illustrating in alphabet books and presentations of familiar literature. Activities in other chapters, for example, writing biographies suggested in Chapter 7 or writing narratives suggested in Chapter 4, also can supply the content for an original picture book.

Making ABC Books

Collect a variety of alphabet books. Originally created to help young children learn to read, this genre seems to pose a challenge to both author and artist as they think of different ways to play with the ABCs. New titles keep appearing, and many are designed for more mature, even adult, readers. Following is a small sample of these books selected to demonstrate the intriguing diversity:

Gathering the Sun: An Alphabet in Spanish and English, written by Alma Flor Ada and illustrated by Simon Silva. Enhanced with strong paintings done in the rich colors of the southwest United States, this bilingual book presents Spanish verses that have been translated into English by Rosa Zubizarreta.

Eye Spy: A Mysterious Alphabet by Linda Bourke. Although this book contains no words, it features wordplay. The reader must examine the four pictures that accompany each letter to determine what sound or meaning they have in common. For example, for *M*, three pictures of monarchs (kings) are followed by a picture of a Monarch butterfly. The letter *Z* is shown with three views of zippers and one picture of a zip code.

A Is for Amos, written by Deborah Chandra and illustrated by Keiko Narahashi. This story is narrated by a horse rider, a young girl named Amos. The book's format provides an interesting challenge for an author.

The Alphabet Soup by Mirko Gabler. This author sets up a brief plot, introducing Gurgla and Blog, twin children of a witch who sent them to school to learn to read. First, the teacher trimmed off their long nails so that they could hold their pencils better, and then she assigned a homework task, making alphabet soup. The twins' ABC recipe begins with Ants, Bagworms, and Crunchy Crabs (they don't care for vegetables like celery). So, the story progresses with high good humor—great for middle schoolers!

A Northern Alphabet by Ted Harrison. Each letter in this book is presented with an alliterative sentence as in "Ff—The frypan will soon fry fish on the flames." The reader is challenged to discover other objects in the illustrations that begin with each letter. Forming a frame for the presentation on each page are names of places in Canada, for example, Fort Nelson, Frobisher Bay, Forty Mile, Fullerton, and Frances Lake. Harrison created an earlier ABC book, *Northland Alphabet*, featuring animals and objects familiar to the Indian and Metis children.

ANTICS! An Alphabetical Anthology by Cathi Hepworth. This is a humorous play on words that contain *ant*. *A*, for example, is for *Antique*, and the illustration depicts a grandmother ant, sitting in a rocking chair on her front porch with a victrola on a nearby stand. All the illustrations show ants in poses relating to the meaning of the word presented—*Flamboyant*, *Observant*, *Tantrum*, and so on.

The Sweet and Sour Animal Book, written by Langston Hughes and illustrated by students from the Harlem School of the Arts. This unpublished manuscript was written by Hughes in 1932 and later discovered. The poems are humorous, and the illustrations, pictures of children's art, are charming. The introduction was written by the poet's friend, Ben Vereen, and the afterword tells about the life of Langston Hughes and how this book was created.

Illuminations by Jonathan Hunt. Each letter in this book is decoratively presented (illuminated) in the tradition of early manuscripts. Each letter also represents a word from medieval times, for example, *B* is for *Black Death*, *N* is for *Normans*, and *T* is for *Troubadour*. A paragraph explains the importance of each word.

Alphabet City by Stephen Johnson. No words appear in this Caldecott Award book. The artist found the letters in surprising places as he traversed New York City. *A*, for instance, is formed by the end of a workman's sawhorse; *E* is formed by the sideview of a traffic light; and *M* is formed by the uprights of the Brooklyn Bridge. Some students might be challenged by this type of treasure hunt with a camera.

Amazon Alphabet, written by Tanis Jordan and illustrated by Martin Jordan. Bold oil paintings often cross two pages in this book to show the plants and animals of the rainforest. The author provides a simple sentence showing each animal in action, for example: *A* is for *Agouti* eating Brazil nuts, and *R* is for *Red Ouakari* leaping through trees. For each animal, the phonetic pronunciation is given so students know how to say the unusual name. This author/illustrator team has traveled extensively in the rainforest and has produced other books such as *Angel Falls: A South American Journey* and *Jungle Days, Jungle Nights*.

Aster Aardvark's Alphabet Adventures by Steven Kellogg. This author/illustrator delights in humorous alliterative sentences. His detailed paintings enhance each crazy creation. He appears to have become worn out at the end, for *Z* includes a picture of zebras cuddled in their blankets on the Sudan with only the expression "Z-Z-Z-Z-Z-Z-Z-Z-Z-Z-Z-Z-Z-Z-Z...."

Alison's Zinnia by Anita Lobel. This artist has painted beautiful flowers for each letter and has created a clever pattern for the text. For the letter *A*, the text reads, "Alison acquired an Amaryllis for Beryl." Notice that this alliterative sentence based on *A* also presents the next letter. For *B*, then, she uses the sentence, "Beryl bought a Begonia for Crystal," and so on. Thus, the book features the names of flowers, verbs, and the names of girls.

On Market Street, written by Arnold Lobel and illustrated by Anita Lobel. Arnold Lobel introduces the art that his wife created for each letter of the alphabet: "I strolled the length of Market Street/To see what I would buy. And I bought...apples, books, clocks, doughnuts, etc." But the pictures are not just of each object, but a human figure created out of, for example, apples, followed by a figure fashioned from books, and then clocks, and doughnuts, and on it goes. Students will be intrigued by this whimsical art.

The Unicorn Alphabet, written by Marianna Mayer and illustrated by Michael Hague. This book centers on figures from the famous medieval Unicorn Tapestries that can be viewed in the Cloisters Museum in New York City. Many of the letters are represented by flowers—columbine, pomegranate, and rose—with explanations of their relationship to the myths of the unicorn. Framing each page is a decoration based on other flowers as explained in the book's glossary. This author/illustrator team also has created *The Unicorn and the Lake,* which retells the legend of the unicorn.

The Birthday ABC, written by Eric Metaxas and illustrated by Tim Raglin. Large pictures depict animals dressed in human clothing in this book. Metaxas has written humorous verses that relate the animal to a birthday celebration. For example, "F is for the *croaking frog,*/muttering upon his log./This day, however, loud and clear,/he croons a song of birthday cheer!"

Ashanti to Zulu: African Traditions, written by Margaret Musgrove and illustrated by Leo and Diane Dillon. This book follows a trend of exploring a single place or topic in dictionary fashion. Much information is presented in short focused paragraphs, and the illustrations by the Dillons are outstanding. Their art won the Caldecott Honor Book award.

Creatures: An Alphabet for Adults and Worldly Children by Frank Newfeld. This Canadian wordless ABC book presents varied illustrations that may intrigue some advanced students. The artist pictures ordinary objects and figures from literature and mythology. An explanation of each plate appears at the back of the book.

A Caribou Alphabet by Mary Beth Owens. Attractive illustrations of caribou surround each large letter in this book. The alphabetic presentation begins with *Antlers,* then *Bulls,* and continues with other words incorporated in sentences that tell about the caribou's life, for example, *grazing, herds,* and *insects.* An afterword further explains the brief information presented with each letter.

Navajo ABC: A Diné Alphabet Book, written by Eleanor Schick and Luci Tapahonso and illustrated by Eleanor Schick. This book features beautiful full-page paintings that focus on a single word, for example, *pottery, uncle,* and *yucca.* A glossary explains the importance of each word in the Diné culture, and the Diné word for each item also is given with phonetic pronunciations.

The Alphabet From Z to A (With Much Confusion on the Way), written by Judith Viorst and illustrated by Richard Hull. This book begins from the front in the usual way, but the author has chosen to present the alphabet backward. She also inserts interesting commentaries about the language. For example, the entry for Z states: "Z is for *ZIP, ZAP,* and *Zero.* But *XYLOPHONE* doesn't (Why not?) start with *Z.*" The illustrations are imaginative, based on words beginning with the letter featured.

A to Zen: A Book of Japanese Culture, written by Ruth Wells and illustrated by Yoshi. In the Japanese custom, this book begins at the back. *A* is for *Aikido*, *B* is for *Bunraku*, and *C* is for *Chanoyu* with each term explained in a short paragraph accompanied by an attractive half-page illustration. This book models a text based on one nation and its culture.

Presenting Familiar Literature

Another kind of picture book that authors and illustrators often present is based on a piece of familiar literature—a poem, a story, or a song. In creating this kind of book students will focus only on the art as they interpret someone else's language. This kind of activity might stimulate extensive reading of poetry, for example, as students decide on a poem to present. Following are picture books that could serve as models for this kind of book:

To Every Thing There Is a Season, illustrated by Leo and Diane Dillon. Here is a truly gorgeous book—eight verses from Ecclesiastes, which form a lovely poem. The Dillons, highly respected artists who have won many awards, have created amazing art representing cultures from all over the world. They explain the style of the art and techniques selected in an afterword.

Cupid and Psyche, retold by Charlotte M. Craft and illustrated by K.Y. Craft. Lavish detailed paintings enhance a retelling of this story from Greek mythology. Talented students might work together to retell a Greek or Roman myth to present as a picture book.

The Owl and the Pussy Cat, written by Edward Lear and illustrated by James Marshall. Marshall died in 1992, so this book was published by his estate with an afterword by noted illustrator and Marshall's friend Maurice Sendak. Sendak describes Marshall's work as "charming nuttiness" characterized by "slap-happiness," which is truly delightful.

The Night Before Christmas, written by Clement C. Moore and illustrated by Tomie dePaola. This familiar poem could be illustrated by a student. Other Christmas songs also might be considered, for example, "Up on the Housetop" or "Jingle Bells."

Connections With Film Art

Students are always interested in films that appear in the theater. Many films are based on classic stories. Other films provide the basis for a picture book that includes art from the film. Examples include the following:

Disney's Mulan, adapted by Kathleen Weidner Zoehfeld and illustrated by Russell Schroeder, tells how this popular animated film was made, beginning with the literary inspiration for the story of Mulan. Photographs show the Asian inspiration for the art used in the film. The film story and sample art are followed by detailed descriptions of what goes on "behind the scenes" concluding with the sections "Computer Animation" and "New Technology." This book will interest students who want to create films. They can investigate further on the Web site www.disneybooks.com. Other versions of the Mulan story are also available: Robert D. San Souci retold *Fa Mulan: The Story of a Woman Warrior*, illustrated by Jean and Mou Sien Tseng; Katherine Poindexter adapted *Disney's Mulan*, illustrated by Jose Cardona and Don Williams.

Adapted by T. Jeanette Steiner and illustrated by Scott Tilley et al., *A Bug's Life: Classic Storybook* includes full-page illustrations from the film. Many students are especially interested in the animation techniques used in this type of film. Students can explore the making of this film further on the Internet at www.disneybooks.com.

Share *The Legend of Sleepy Hollow*, which some students may have seen interpreted in film. One picture book is *The Legend of Sleepy Hollow*, retold by Robert D. San Souci and illustrated by Daniel San Souci. Another version is *Glenn Close Reads The Legend of Sleepy Hollow*, a video with music by Tim Story.

See also the discussion of *Star Wars* in Chapter 7.

Involving Students With Music

Like art, music may engage student interest in other curricular studies. Picture books may serve as an introduction to a creative study that involves history or multicultural concerns. Students will enjoy singing songs relating to their studies, setting poetry or prose to music, or even choreographing a presentation to share with other classes. Following are a few books to explore.

Songs to Sing

A particularly impressive picture book is *This Land Is Your Land* based on words and music by Woody Guthrie first sung in 1940. Illustrations by Kathy Jakobsen, ending with a three-page spread, depict the words of this favorite song that fits so well with efforts to achieve equitable treatment for all in the United States. An afterword tells about the life of this guitarist and singer who tried valiantly to improve the conditions of factory workers and opportunities for migrants. "A

Tribute to Woody Guthrie" by his friend Pete Seeger, and the full text for Woody's song, conclude the book. Students will enjoy singing this song for an assembly, perhaps accompanied by a guitar.

Students who want to work with young children as a service project should know old favorite songs such as "The Farmer in the Dell," which is the basis for an enjoyable game that gets all the children in a group involved. Illustrated with primitive-style art by Alexandra Wallner, *The Farmer in the Dell* is another example of the kind of book students also might create. Both words and music are included in the book.

Sarah Josepha Hale's familiar rhyme is illustrated by Tomie dePaola as *Mary Had a Little Lamb*. Students could follow this model to produce a book based on a Mother Goose rhyme or other familiar jingle.

Another favorite with children is "I Know an Old Lady Who Swallowed a Fly," a song older students can teach youngsters with the aid of flannel board figures. An attractive edition of this song is retold and illustrated by Nadine Bernard Westcott.

Lullabies also suggest music your students can sing with elementary school children. The traditional lullaby *All the Pretty Little Horses* has been illustrated by Linda Saport. Another collection of lullabies is *Ocean Lullabies and Night Verses*, compiled and illustrated by Kate Kiesler.

Featuring People From the World of Music

Biographies or stories about the lives of musicians, singers, and dancers make the individuals come alive for students. Students who have special interest in music will enjoy exploring some of the following picture books.

The life of black modern dance artist Alvin Ailey is presented in an attractive book titled *Alvin Ailey* by Andrea Davis Pinkney. The illustrations by the author's husband, Brian Pinkney, are beautiful scratch etchings that are especially appropriate to show the powerful movements of the dancers.

Talented artist Jeanette Winter wrote and illustrated *Sebastian: A Book about Bach*. Winter includes intriguing facts that will engage students' interest; for example, a recording of Bach's music was carried aboard the first Voyager spacecraft.

Richard Tames wrote about Chopin, noted French pianist and composer, in *Frederic Chopin*. This volume is illustrated with historic photographs that provide a sense of history.

Roland Vernon wrote a biography of a more contemporary composer, George Gershwin, *Introducing Gershwin*. This book, too, is illustrated with photographs.

Check your library shelves for other biographies or stories about noted musicians that meet your needs.

Fiction Featuring Music

Sometimes music is an important factor in a narrative. This may appeal to students who are involved with music. It also may help you reach a reluctant reader.

Mentioned in Chapter 6, *The Cello of Mr. O* is about a musician who becomes a hero when he plays his beautiful cello in the middle of the square to help his neighbors cope with the fears of war. When his cello is destroyed by bombs, he returns with a harmonica and continues playing.

The Bat Boy & His Violin, written by Gavin Curtis and illustrated by E.B. Lewis, combines two themes: playing the violin and the role of African Americans in early baseball history. Reginald's father manages the worst baseball team in the Negro National League. Thinking his son spends too much time indoors, he appoints him bat boy for the Dukes. He does not appreciate his son's musical talents until the boy's music energizes the players so much that they win their first game in months.

A funny book that incorporates music and would be great to share with primary-grade students is *Animal Music*, written by Harriet Ziefert and illustrated by Donald Saaf: "Goat plays banjo,/Cat plays fiddle./All the dancers/Crowd to the middle." Young children would enjoy acting out this story as it is read aloud. They could strut around the room parade-fashion with Mr. Lions Marching Band. The bold, colorful art also might suggest painting a class mural with younger children.

A Russian folk tale that features the music of a gusli (little harp) is *Music of the Tsar of the Sea*, retold by Celia Barker Lottridge and illustrated with mysterious paintings by Harvey Chan. Sadko, a poor minstrel, is given rich jewels in return for his music to which the tsar and his guests dance. When he visits the tsar's palace at the bottom of the Caspian Sea, he meets the tsar's daughter, Volkova, who returns to Earth with him in the form of the Volga River.

Quite a different book is *Swan Lake*, a classic tale retold by Mark Helprin and illustrated beautifully by Chris Van Allsburg. This is the tale of a young girl and her grandfather who live in the forest high on the mountainside. He tells her the story of her parents, Odette and the son of the Emperor, whom he tutored. A group of students could research this tale and listen to Tchaikovsky's music created for the ballet of *Swan Lake*. Perhaps they could devise an interesting way to share their findings with others in the class. When they are familiar with the story of

Swan Lake, students might enjoy the spoof presented in *Honk!*, written by Pamela Edwards and illustrated by Henry Cole. Mimi, a swan, always wanted to be a prima swanerina, and she repeatedly tries to see a production of *Swan Lake*. Finally, she manages to get on the stage with the other dancers and makes quite a hit!

As pointed out earlier in this chapter, *No Mirrors in My Nana's House* by Ysaye M. Barnwell includes a CD-ROM on which the author's words are sung. Students might like to provide musical accompaniment to the reading of a picture book they especially like.

Dance is featured in *My Mama Had a Dancing Heart*, written by Libba Moore Gray and illustrated by Raul Colon. Poetic language tells of the shared experiences of a mother and daughter. The daughter remembers those days as she prepares to perform a ballet.

Another picture book that features dance is Ruth Bornstein's *The Dancing Man*. Joseph, a young orphan boy who lives in a village on the shores of the Baltic Sea, dances beside the sea. Bornstein's beautiful large pastel paintings complete the story effectively.

Conclusion

In Chapter 8 we have examined picture books that may stimulate student creativity in art or music. I introduced a number of books that have won the Caldecott Award and suggested studies of the art in children's literature. Activities related to featured titles were designed to engage middle school students in creating art and in making original children's books. Throughout the chapter I attempted to point out connections between the illustrations in picture books and film art and music. In Chapter 9 we will investigate the use of picture books as launching pads for theme studies.

Wilfrid Gordon McDonald Partridge

Written by Mem Fox   Illustrated by Julie Vivas

First published in America in 1985 by Kane/Miller Book Publishers, Brooklyn, New York. Originally published in Australia in 1984 by Omnibus Books. Text ©1984 Mem Fox. Illustrations ©1984 Julie Vivas.

CHAPTER 9

Introducing Thematic Studies

An exciting way to teach at any level is through a thematic study or unit. Teachers of all ability levels can find suitable activities and resources relating to a broad theme so students can participate in meaningful learning. The picture book often can provide an introduction to units of study on self–identity, conflict, family, intergenerational relations, gender, stereotypes, diversity, and immigration.

Theme 1: Inner Space or Getting to Know Yourself

The popular theme of "Getting to Know Yourself" is sometimes associated with self–identity. It should be a good study for middle school students as they work through these transitional years of their lives. Introduce this topic by focusing on autobiographical material in picture books, perhaps something that emphasizes memories of childhood. Reading these books may suggest various ways for students to begin their own narratives and different kinds of content to include. The following picture books, which are mainly autobiographical, could be used for this purpose:

On the Bus with Joanna Cole: A Creative Autobiography by Joanna Cole with Wendy Saul. This book is part of a publisher's series called Creative Sparks, which features authors and illustrators that might interest you and your students. Many students may know Joanna Cole's books about the Magic School Bus, which present science in an inviting way. In this book she tells about her own life, why she writes, and where she gets her ideas.

In Flight With David McPhail: A Creative Autobiography by David McPhail. This is another book in the Creative Sparks series. This author/illustrator informs readers about his work in a scrapbook-type format that may suggest ideas for young writers.

When I Was Young in the Mountains by Cynthia Rylant pictures the author's memories of living in West Virginia with her grandparents; her grandfather was a coal miner.

Wilfrid Gordon McDonald Partridge by Mem Fox. This story, mentioned in Chapter 6, is about an elderly woman who has lost her memory. Young Wilfrid tries to find his friend's memory. It is interesting to observe what he discovers to re-create her memory.

The All-New Amelia by Marissa Moss. Amelia writes and illustrates a journal that discusses what is happening in her life. There are also additional Amelia books. This fictionalized writing will suggest ideas for students.

From the Hills of Georgia: An Autobiography in Paintings by Mattie Lou O'Kelly. The brightly colored paintings in this book depict life in the early 20th century beginning with the author's birth at home with the whole family awaiting the arrival of another baby.

A Christmas Memory, written by Truman Capote and illustrated by Beth Peck. This charming autobiographical Christmas story tells about a little boy who helps his eccentric aunt make fruitcake, an annual tradition. This is another picture book written by an author who is best known for adult literature.

Thinking + Lesson Plan 14 in Appendix A (see page 155) guides middle school students to write autobiographical essays based on their memories.

Theme II: The Quilt: A Metaphor for Our Multicultural Society

The patchwork quilt is a wonderful metaphor for a multicultural society like that in the United States. Quilts have played an important role in the history of the United States. A number of authors and illustrators focus on the quilt in picture books that can be used to introduce this theme.

Sweet Clara and the Freedom Quilt, written by Deborah Hopkinson and illustrated by James Ransome, tells the story of Clara, a young slave girl who is separated from her mother. A kindly woman teaches her to sew to save her from the drudgery of the cotton fields. She begins to work in the Big House where she overhears talk of runaway slaves. Someone says, "It'd be easy if you had a map." Clara gradually learns about Canada and the way to freedom, and she stitches a map in her quilt for others to follow.

Eleanor Coerr relates another quilt story in *The Josefina Story Quilt*, illustrated by Bruce Degen. This easy-to-read book offers a good way for ESL students to participate in a theme study focusing on the quilt. Faith sews a patchwork quilt to record the happenings while enroute west on a wagon train. Josefina is Faith's pet hen that causes nothing but trouble until the night her cackling warns them of robbers. When Josefina dies, Faith makes a special quilt square in honor of her pet.

Artist Faith Ringgold creates amazing story quilts that hang on the wall. Composed collage-fashion, they are decorated with quotations and framed with quilt blocks. One of her story quilts has been developed into a book titled *Tar Beach*, mentioned in a previous chapter.

Other books featuring quilts and quilting include the following:

A Name on the Quilt: A Story of Remembrance, written by Jeannine Atkins and illustrated by Tad Hills. In this story a family creates a quilt in honor of a family member who has died of AIDS.

The Patchwork Quilt, written by Valerie Flournoy and illustrated by Jerry Pinkney. In this book Tanya finishes the quilt her African American grandmother was too ill to complete.

The Log Cabin Quilt by Ellen Howard. The mother's quilt scraps are used as chinking between the logs to keep the family warm in Howard's book, thus creating an unusual kind of quilt on the walls.

The Keeping Quilt by Patricia Polacco. This author/illustrator traces her Jewish heritage in a quilt made from family clothing.

Other resource books about quilting that might be useful include Raymond Bial's *With Needle and Thread: A Book About Quilts* and Mary Cobb's *The Quilt Block History of Pioneer Days*.

In addition, several gifted students might research quilting by the Amish people, quilting in Hawaii, and African American quilts. The lesson in Thinking + Lesson Plan 15 in Appendix A (see page 156) focuses on creating a quilt as a class project.

Theme III: Immigrants and Immigration

Immigration is a timely topic for study because there seems to be renewed concern about the numbers of new people entering the United States and their impact, for example, on public schools. Stories can help students better understand the feelings of the immigrants who arrive in a new country.

Riki Levinson has written several books about children who enter the United States as immigrants. The first is *Watch the Stars Come Out*, illustrated by Diane Goode, in which a grandmother relates the experience of coming to the United States as a child with her 10-year-old brother on a ship that took 23 days to cross the Atlantic. At last the children were released to their parents to begin a new life in New York City. The illustrations are especially well-done portrayals of the children's experiences. A second book by Levinson is *Soon, Annala* with pictures by Julie Downing. This book continues Levinson's first story with the arrival of the two youngest children traveling with their aunt and uncle. On the day their ship docked, Annala and her family wait eagerly as ferry after ferry comes from Ellis Island. Finally, the family is united.

A fine immigrant story is presented by Eve Bunting in *How Many Days to America?: A Thanksgiving Story*, illustrated by Beth Peck. Here again the emphasis is on the length of the trip and the experience of arriving in a new country. However, Bunting ties her story into the Thanksgiving holiday as people welcome the newcomers and celebrate together.

The story of an immigrant told in the first person, *When I First Came to This Land* is based on an old folk poem retold by Harriet Ziefert with pictures by award-winning artist Simms Taback. Written in fascinating cumulative verse form, this book suggests language activities that might augment autobiograpical writing based on memories. The book also could be used to focus on the artist's work because the double-page spreads are very impressive. A lesson based on this story is presented in Thinking + Lesson Plan 16 in Appendix A (see page 157).

Immigrant Kids by Russell Freedman is another informative book about the lives of immigrant children. This nonfiction work is illustrated with photographs showing children at play, but more often at work, for their life was not easy as they helped earn the family living. Yet they were happy to be free in the United States with their families.

Theme IV: Love

Love is an important theme, but may require a little finesse to approach with middle school students. Picture books that talk about love between an animal parent and its offspring may help students discuss the need for love that we all share.

One book that presents a loving relationship is Martin Waddell's *Who Do You Love?*, illustrated by Camilla Ashforth. Here we see a cat named Holly exhibiting all the behaviors of a human child. The kitten plays a game with her mother as she gets Holly ready for bed, enumerating all the people she loves in response to her mother's question, "Who do you love, Holly?" Of course, she names everyone but her mother, but that's part of the game, too, as the mother cat pretends to cry until Holly responds, "I love you." The mother cat responds, "I love you, too. You know that I do," and tucks her into her blanket. The illustrations are soft and attractive, fitting the mood of the story.

In *How Long?* by Elizabeth Dale, Alan Marks's charming paintings help tell the story of a mouse and her mother. Caroline always wanted to know "how long," which she learns to define in her own terms. Finally she asks, "How long will you love me for?" Her mother replies, "As long as it took to make all the stars in the sky and the moon and everything else there is." Still the mouse is worried that her mother will then stop loving her, but her mother makes clear that she will "have only just begun!"

In Miela Ford's *Mom and Me*, the love is expressed between a polar bear cub and its mother. Pictures are charming with very simple language. This is another good book for ESL students.

I Love You the Purplest, written by Barbara Joosse and illustrated by Mary Whyte, depicts a single mother and her two sons who set out to fish on the lake near their cabin. The author details an interesting contrast between the two boys and their behavior. Then they begin vying for their mother's approval and finally, her love. "Mama, who do you love best?" they ask in turn as they get into bed. Their mother tells each one of her love creatively: "Why, Julian, I love you the bluest! I love you the color of a dragon fly at the tip of its wing" and "Why Max, I love you the reddest! I love you the color of the sky before it blazes into night." The boys are satisfied.

Paul Zindel's charming book *I Love My Mother*, illustrated by John Melo, is largely autobiographical. As a boy, he was raised by his mother whom he obviously appreciates very much.

Another kind of love is described in Shel Silverstein's *The Giving Tree*. The tree gives and gives, and the boy takes and takes. The boy says he loves the tree, but his is a very selfish kind of love. Students might compare the kinds of love described in this book with that in another book about a loving relationship, as in Thinking + Lesson Plan 17, in Appendix A (see page 158).

Additional books that feature varied kinds of love include these:

Bigmama's by Donald Crews

Abuela, written by Arthur Dorros and illustrated by Elisa Kleven

A Bedtime Story, written by Joan Goldman Levine and illustrated by Gail Owens

Mrs. Katz and Tush by Patricia Polacco

Back Home, written by Gloria Jean Pinkney and illustrated by Jerry Pinkney

Introducing Other Themes With Picture Books

Here are a number of suggestions for other themes you might explore with an introduction by a picture book or two.

Death and Grieving

Some students may have experienced the death of a close friend or relative and have gone through the grieving process. Reading fiction about the experiences of others may help students share their emotions. With text by Dorothy Carter and illustrations by Harvey Stevenson, *Bye, Mis' Lela* is an attractive picture book about this topic. A child learns about remembering an old friend who has died. She joins the adults at the wake to say a final good-bye. The child remembers her friend's warm words and continues to say, "Bye, Mis' Lela" as she passes her house.

The Elderly

Many students do not have direct contact with older people. A study focusing on the increasing percentage of elderly people in society could help students gain greater empathy for people past 70 years old. In Leyla Torres's *Liliana's Grandmothers*, Liliana has two quite different grandmothers. One lives just down the street in New England and the other lives in South America. Liliana visits them both and notices the differences between them. However, the main thing is that both are warm and loving. This story is an excellent example of contrast.

As part of a study about the elderly, students could visit a nursing home or invite grandparents who live in the vicinity to come to school to talk with them. Another charming book about the elderly is Mem Fox's *Wilfrid Gordon McDonald Partridge* (illustrated on page 128). Wilfrid searches for Miss Nancy's lost memory.

Slavery

Alan Schroeder has written an outstanding book about Harriet Tubman titled *Minty: A Story of Young Harriet Tubman*, illustrated with striking paintings by Jerry Pinkney. This fictional account of the rebellious young girl's early years is based on facts. Both author and illustrator reveal the fear and physical abuse the child, christened Araminta, suffered on the Brodas plantation in Maryland. It was this experience that drove Tubman to flee from slavery. Other stories tell of her heroic efforts to lead other slaves to freedom.

The Desire for Freedom

Books about slavery and the African Americans' flight to freedom (see Chapter 6) come immediately to mind when the theme of "The Desire for Freedom" is mentioned. The stories of immigrants also fit in this theme. A more unusual book about the desire for freedom is *The Big Box*, written by Toni Morrison and her son, Slade Morrison, and illustrated by Giselle Potter. The authors make a commentary about the boxes parents put their children in. The parents give the children food, shelter, and entertainment and put them safely in a big box, saying "You can't handle freedom." However, they schedule only a few visits each week to spend time with their children. No wonder the children try to escape from the box!

The Settling of the Western United States

Holling Clancy Holling's wonderful book *Tree in the Trail* was published years ago, but it provides an amazing overview of the interaction of American Indians, white settlers, explorers, and hunters in the Kansas and Missouri territory. In the book, mentioned in Chapter 5, a tree grows over the years observing the action that passes beside and then beneath it. Standing in one place for 200 years, it collects souvenirs from the various persons who pass by. When it dies it finally moves from its place beside the trail and becomes an impressive yoke for a team of oxen.

Something Beautiful

It is important to take time to appreciate the beauty in the world. Barbara Cooney writes and illustrates a story titled *Miss Rumphius*, which tells us that one of our goals in life should be to create something beautiful. Another interesting picture book that deals with this topic is *What's the Most Beautiful Thing You Know About Horses?*, written by Richard Van Camp and illustrated by George Littlechild. These books could initiate a study of people who have been driven to create something beautiful. Students can then consider what they can do to make the world more beautiful. This study might suggest a class project.

Passion

What do you care about more than anything else in the world? Do you have a passion? Winner of the 1999 Caldecott Award, artist Mary Azarian was attracted to the manuscript for *Snowflake Bentley*, written by Jacqueline Briggs Martin, because Wilson Bentley "was a person who had a small focused passion that he pursued his whole life." Author Jacqueline Martin chose to write about this little-known Vermont man who from boyhood was fascinated by snowflakes. He was determined to photograph their beauty. Students could discuss someone they know who has such a passion, or perhaps they have a passion themselves. This study could focus on inventors, explorers, artists, writers, and so on, persons who have a drive to discover or to create something new.

Gods and Goddesses

When we think of gods and goddesses, we usually think of famous Greek and Roman figures from mythology. Students could broaden their knowledge by learning about mythology from other cultures, for example, Scandinavia, Asia, and India. A story from India's great national epic *The Mahabharata* might be used to introduce such an exploratory venture. *Savitri: A Tale of Ancient India*, retold by Aaron Shepard and illustrated by Vera Rosenberry, tells of great love and exemplifies courage, wit, and strong determination. The author/illustrator team Ingri and Edgar Parin d'Aulaire produced some attractive and informative picture books about mythology, for example, *Norse Gods and Giants* and *Book of Greek Myths*.

Native Americans Today and Yesterday

Students know little about the many tribes that lived in the United States at the time Columbus landed on the North American continent. They know even less about the Native Americans and their lives today. You might begin a study of this group of Americans with a picture book such as *Thirteen Moons on Turtle's Back: A Native American Year of Moons*, written by Joseph Bruchac and Jonathan London and illustrated by Thomas Locker. This collection of poems is based on Indian legends, emphasizing the story associated with each of the 13 moons. Another good choice would be one of Paul Goble's many fine books about Native Americans. For example, in *The Legend of the White Buffalo Woman*, mentioned in Chapter 6, Goble tells the story of a beautiful young woman who symbolizes the harmony between the Indian and the buffalo. Recognizing the sense of kinship Indians hold for the buffalo, this story tells how they came to be related. Another fine artist/author is Gerald McDermott, whose beautiful picture book *Raven: A Trickster Tale from the Pacific Northwest* is an excellent example of lore from the Native American culture.

Disabilities and How People Cope With Them

Students could benefit from learning about various disabilities as a way of increasing empathy for those who are less able. A charming picture book about a deaf girl, *Mandy* by Barbara Booth and Jim Lamarche could serve to introduce this theme. This story shares the thoughts and feelings of young Amanda, who has "never heard anyone talk or sing." *Sound of Sunshine, Sound of Rain* by Florence Heide, mentioned earlier, is a fine book about a blind child who is particularly optimistic. Students could find nonfiction, too, that would increase their understanding about specific disabilities.

The Days of Long Ago

Students can perhaps imagine the days of long ago through stories they hear from grandparents. A picture book like *Granddaddy's Street Songs*, written by Monalisa DeGross and illustrated by Floyd Cooper, introduces this kind of history. In this case the grandfather tells what life was like for him in the early days of Baltimore, Maryland. This lyrical writing focuses on the interesting feature that was common in most towns, the street vendors who drove a horse and wagon through the streets calling out their wares: "Listen to me sing, listen to me holler./Listen while I tell you what I got for a dollar." Students might enjoy trying the calls included in this attractive book. Here is an interesting way to engage students in a story of what life was like in the early 1900s when their grandparents were young. This book also fits with the theme on "The Elderly" suggested earlier.

Celebrations

I'm in Charge of Celebrations, a marvelous book written by Byrd Baylor and illustrated by Peter Parnall, would be perfect to initiate a celebration theme. Another picture book that features a celebration, a birthday party with no presents, is *Three Cheers for Catherine the Great!*, written by Cari Best and illustrated by Giselle Potter. The family members are challenged to think of how to honor the grandmother, a Russian immigrant who does not want presents on her birthday. Students might think, as this family did, about the things that really matter compared to all the things we usually give and receive for special occasions.

Changing Stereotyped Thinking

As discussed in the section "Exploring Stereotyped Thinking" in Chapter 6, it is important to discuss this topic in the classroom to help students understand and appreciate diversity. A picture book that presents obvious stereotypes that students can readily identify is *Sylvester and the Magic Pebble*, written and illustrated by William Steig. This fantasy tells of a donkey family, the Duncans, and what happened when their son, Sylvester, found a magic pebble. The stereotypes are not in the text but in the illustrations. On the first page, for instance, Sylvester and his parents are shown in the living room. Father Duncan is sitting in an easy chair smoking and reading the newspaper, while Mother Duncan, wearing an apron, is sweeping the floor with a broom. When Sylvester is lost, his parents go to the police station, and in this illustration the policemen are pictured as pigs. (Interestingly, this book won the 1970 Caldecott Award for its illustrations.) Here is a perfect example of how thinking has changed about the role of women in our society. Have students discuss why the way we portray women in books and films or how we use language matters. They can bring in examples of stereotypes or of changed thinking from the newspaper or share things that they hear in the street or see on television. The Caldecott Award book *Smoky Night*, written by Eve Bunting and illustrated by David Diaz, offers a wonderful example of how thinking can change. (See also the lesson on this topic referred to in Chapter 6.)

Women and Their Contributions

William Miller has done an extraordinary job of telling a story about one segment of a person's life in a way that helps readers understand the person's life. One example of his work is *Zora Hurston and the Chinaberry Tree*, illustrated by Cornelius Van Wright and Ying-Hwa Hu. This inspirational story, mentioned in Chapter 6, focuses on one episode in this noted African American writer's life. Richard Dungworth wrote and illustrated *The Usborne Book of Famous Women*, which introduces a number of women who warrant further research.

Conclusion

In this final chapter we have explored possibilities for using picture books as launching pads for thematic units that cross the curriculum. The four major themes that I developed more fully include Self-Identity, The Quilt as a Metaphor for Our Multiculture, Immigrants and Immigration, and Love. In addition, I suggested ways of approaching 14 other themes that might initiate interesting studies in the middle school. Having concluded the final chapter, I leave you now with a short afterword.

fterword

So, we have come full cycle in our exploration of picture books that can be used to enhance teaching in the middle school. I hope you have enjoyed our journey together.

My hope is that you will continue to explore the thousands of picture books that are available to you in local libraries and bookstores. Remember, too, that some 3,000 new picture books will be published each year.

Much as you might develop a stock portfolio to increase your personal wealth, begin now to compile a portfolio of ideas and books that will enrich your particular curriculum. Buy that copy of Mother Goose rhymes, a few choice humorous stories, and of course, several books that are illustrated by outstanding artists. Your investment of time and money will repay you handsomely.

Join me and the many fine authors and artists who have chosen picture books as a way of touching the lives of young people. Join people like talented writer Eloise Greenfield, who said the following to a group of teachers attending the International Reading Association Convention in 1975:

> I want to encourage children to develop positive attitudes toward themselves and their abilities.... I want to write stories that will allow children to fall in love with Black heroes and in dedication to the cause of Black freedom.... I want to be one of those who can choose and order words that children will want to celebrate. I want to make them shout and laugh and blink back tears and care about themselves. They are our future.

If you would like to share your ideas, you can e-mail me at irismt@worldnet.att.net. I'd love to hear from you.

Join the celebration!

Lesson Plans

Thinking + Lesson Plan 1
Title of Lesson: Exploring the Concept of Stewardship

Expected Outcomes

The learner will

1. read a story that explains stewardship.
2. summarize the importance of stewardship in our lives.
3. write a personal plan for being a good steward.
4. share this information with others.

Teaching/Learning Strategy

Resources: Obtain at least one copy of *Stuartship* by Ryan Collay and Joanne Dubrow.

Directions

Step I: Read *Stuartship* aloud to the class. Stop to have students answer the questions posed periodically throughout the book. Discuss the concept of stewardship. Have the class compose a definition of stewardship and suggest related synonyms.

Step II: Have students work in cooperative learning groups to compile a list of ways in which they individually might help take better care of our planet.

Step III: Have each student enter an individual pledge in his or her writing journal stating personal plans for carrying out stewardship.

Assessment Performance

1. Students will plan a brief performance to share with other classes. This might include Readers Theatre, a short skit, or transparencies. One or more students can introduce different parts of the presentation. Students also can be selected to serve as the director or producer of the production.

2. Gifted students can prepare a multimedia presentation to share with their own class and others.

3. This whole program can be presented to the Parent Teacher Association as an effort to inform the community about an important issue.

As you develop similar lessons and projects with colleagues, you may want to create activity sheets that can be duplicated for student use or placed on a transparency. As you talk about the books you have read and your lesson ideas, each of you may add suggestions for amplifying the presentations.

Thinking + Lesson Plan 2
Title of Lesson: Reading "Jack and Jill"

Expected Outcomes

The learner will

1. listen to "Jack and Jill" read aloud on a tape.
2. follow the spoken words on a printed copy.
3. read the poem independently.

Teaching/Learning Strategy

Resources: Set up a listening center for 6–10 students. Tape "Jack and Jill," repeating it several times. Speak slowly and clearly. Make printed copies of the poem. This is an excellent activity for an aide to supervise.

Directions

Step I: Have students listen to the taped poem "Jack and Jill." An aide can ask students the following questions (or tape them):
           Who are Jack and Jill? (a little boy and girl)
           What did they do? (went up a hill to get water)
           What happened? (Jack fell down and hurt his head. Jill fell down, too.)
           Explain any words that may give difficulty such as *fetch, pail, crown,* or *tumbling;* you may include simple drawings on the printed copy of the poem to assist understanding. After discussing the meaning, listen to the poem again.

Step II: Give each student a printed copy of the poem. Direct them to point to each word as the speaker says it on the tape. (Directions can be included on the tape.) Students should repeat this step at least two or three times.

Step III: Have the students read the poem aloud with the speaker at least twice. Then have them try reading the poem independently. At this stage it is acceptable if they repeat the rhyme from memory instead of actually reading it.

Assessment Performance

1. Observe students reading aloud with the tape.
2. Have students read the poem aloud on a tape or to an aide or another student.

Thinking + Lesson Plan 3
Title of Lesson: A Readers Theatre Presentation of *Little Red Riding Hood*

Expected Outcomes

The learner will

1. read at least one version of *Little Red Riding Hood*.
2. collaborate on scripting the story for presentation.
3. participate in presenting the story as Readers Theatre.

Teaching/Learning Strategy

Resources: Obtain at least one version of *Little Red Riding Hood*. Recommended: *Little Red Riding Hood*, retold and illustrated by Trina Schart Hyman, which won the Caldecott Award.

Directions

Be aware that methods of working with Readers Theatre differ. Directions given here follow one accepted method. Duplicate at least five copies of the text so that students can mark the copy or cut it up, as needed.

Step I: Show students how to identify the exact words that a character says and how to eliminate the "he saids" or "she saids" as in this line: "Yes, Mama," *said Little Red Riding Hood*. "I promise. I will do just as you tell me."

As they learn to script, students will observe how quotation marks are used to set off the words as each character speaks. They will cross out the unnecessary words printed in italicized letters in the previous line from *Little Red Riding Hood*.

After rereading the story, students should list the characters that appear, that is, the roles to be read. They also can decide what essential background information needs to be provided (taken directly from the text) by a narrator. You may encourage them to choose more than one narrator, thus providing for more participants. The narrator sets the stage, as in this excerpt:

Once upon a time, there was a little girl named Elisabeth who lived with her mother in a house on the edge of a village....

Step II: Prepare the script with the words for each role clearly stated. Make copies of the prepared script so that each reader has a copy. The scripts are often placed within black covers that do not detract from the presentation. Often the speakers sit on simple stools. They may sit on plain chairs, standing up only when they read their parts. Usually, there is no attempt to use props or costumes for a Readers Theatre presentation, but methods vary. In any case, the focus should remain on reading well and presenting the story so the audience can understand it.

Step III: Practice reading the story aloud with each person reading his or her role, as assigned. Have persons serve as director and producer of the presentation. They may make suggestions about the delivery of the lines. They also may suggest the need for added words to clarify the story for the audience or to make the roles more interesting. Encourage students to play with such embellishments as choruses or the repetition of lines for emphasis.

Assessment Performance

1. Observe student participation in the preparation process. They can receive a + or - depending on whether they participate at least minimally.

2. Each student should perform at least one time in a given role. Making an effort to perform adequately will constitute a "Pass" or + score. Two students can be selected to make these assessments using a prepared checklist. (Rotate these positions.)

Thinking + Lesson Plan 3. *Teaching With Picture Books in the Middle School* by Iris McClellan Tiedt, ©2000 International Reading Association. May be copied.

Thinking + Lesson Plan 4
Title of Lesson: The Library

Expected Outcomes

The learner will

1. read a story about Richard Wright and his library card.
2. visit the local library and obtain a library card.
3. write a paragraph about what libraries have to offer.

Teaching/Learning Strategy

Resources: Obtain a copy of William Miller's picture book *Richard Wright and the Library Card*.

Directions

Step I: Read this short book aloud and ask students to listen empathetically. (If students don't know the word *empathy*, make a point of introducing this word prior to this lesson.) They are to try to put themselves in Wright's shoes as they share his feelings.

Step II: Ask students to write questions about this story that begin with the following words:
1. Who…
2. What…
3. Where…
4. When…
5. Why…
Then students can ask one another these questions in small groups as a stimulus to discussing the story.

Step III: Have a group of gifted students research Richard Wright and report their findings to the class.

Step IV: Schedule a trip to the local library. See that students are able to get their own library card if they do not have one.

Assessment Performance

1. Students will write a paragraph about what libraries have to offer.
2. Students will use their library cards for future class activities.

Thinking + Lesson Plan 5
Title of Lesson: The Pourquoi Tale

Expected Outcomes

The learner will

1. read a number of pourquoi tales.

2. write a pourquoi tale that explains a natural phenomenon.

Teaching/Learning Strategies

Resources: Collect a number of folk tales that explain why something has happened—pourquoi tales. One especially good book to use is *Tikki Tikki Tembo*, a story retold by Arlene Mosel and illustrated by Blair Lent.

Directions

Step I: Each day for a week read aloud one pourquoi tale. Following the reading begin a list of the characteristics of a pourquoi tale. Add new items to the list as appropriate.

Step II: Brainstorm a list of events that could possibly be explained in a pourquoi tale, such as the following:
Why cats tend to have blue or greenish eyes.
Why we sleep at night instead of in the daytime.
Why we use a sheep's wool to make cloth.
Remember that any suggestions are accepted in brainstorming. Have two or more students write this list on the chalkboard to keep track of the ideas.

Step III: Have students choose one of the ideas listed as the subject for creating an original pourquoi tale.

Assessment Performance

1. Have students work in pairs to edit and revise their stories. Final versions can be read aloud in small groups.

2. Prepare a class book of these tales.

Thinking + Lesson Plan 5. *Teaching With Picture Books in the Middle School* by Iris McClellan Tiedt, ©2000 International Reading Association. May be copied.

Thinking + Lesson Plan 6
Title of Lesson: Discovering the Metaphor

Expected Outcomes

The learner will

1. read a poem that contains a metaphor.
2. write a short poem that expresses a metaphor.

Teaching/Learning Strategy

Resources: Locate a copy of Emily Dickinson's "I Like to See It Lap the Miles."

Directions

Step I: Give each student a copy of Dickinson's poem or display it on a transparency. Read the poem aloud. Read it a second time, asking students to think about what picture comes to mind as they listen. Then, ask students what the poet is writing about. (Not all students will know, but usually one will suggest a train.) Then, guide the students to pick out words that make them think of trains. Note that the poet never uses the word *train* specifically.

Ask students what the poet compares the train to, and have them identify the words that tell them that. You might have someone look up the reference to Boanerges in mythology.

Explain that the poet could have said, "A train is like a horse" (a simile) or "A train is a horse" (a metaphor), but she chose to be more subtle by creating an extended metaphor that suggests that idea in a more creative way.

Step II: Have students brainstorm a series of possible metaphors by linking a noun from the following List 1 with a noun in List 2 or vice versa. Add words to the lists freely as ideas occur. Use the following format: (A) _____ is (a) _____.

List 1

smile	book	red
cat	wing	silver
house	spoon	apple
chain	song	peace
ring	ruler	fog
road	love	beauty
frog		

List 2

rock	person	purple
pencil	guardian	moon
tree	table	treasure
automobile	hug	friend
flower	present	power
cloud	freedom	dog
star		

Ask each student to choose one relationship to develop as a metaphor in poetry or prose, trying to extend the image as much as possible.

Assessment Performance

Students will illustrate their metaphors and display them on the classroom wall.

Thinking + Lesson Plan 7
Title of Lesson: Writing Fabulous Fables

Expected Outcomes

The learner will

    1. read a number of fables.

    2. identify the characteristics of a fable.

    3. write original fables.

Teaching/Learning Strategy

Resources: Duplicate copies of three Aesop fables for each student.

Directions

Step I: Have students work in cooperative learning groups to read the fables together.

Step II: Have each group make a list of the characteristics of a fable based on those they have read. They will share their lists with the class to compile a list they can all use.

Step III: Have students work in pairs to write a fable that contains the characteristics agreed on.

Assessment Performance

    1. Students will read their fables aloud to the class. The class will check off the characteristics of a fable that are included.

    2. The class will publish a collection of their best fables to put in the school library.

Thinking + Lesson Plan 7. *Teaching With Picture Books in the Middle School* by Iris McClellan Tiedt, ©2000 International Reading Association. May be copied.

Thinking + Lesson Plan 8
Title of Lesson: Thinking About Esteem

Expected Outcomes

The learner will

1. listen to a story about self-esteem.
2. discuss questions about the character development.
3. write a paragraph about the importance of having self-esteem.

Teaching/Learning Strategy

Resources: Obtain a copy of *Willy the Wimp* by Anthony Browne.

Directions

Step I: Read the book aloud to the class showing them the pictures of Willy.

Step II: Then, ask some of the following questions:
1. Why do you think Willy always says, "I'm sorry." (Give students time to think.)
   Example: His mother told him always to be polite.
2. Why did the author choose to end the story with that funny incident?
   Example: She was trying to remind us to be humble.

Step III: Discuss self-esteem: What is it? Why is it important? How do other people affect our self-esteem?

Assessment Performance

Have students write a paragraph in their journals on why self-esteem is important.

Thinking + Lesson Plan 9
Title of Lesson: The Dimensions of Friendship

Expected Outcomes

The learner will

1. list the qualities that make a good friend.
2. read books about different kinds of friends.
3. write a short essay on the topic "What Friendship Means to Me."

Teaching/Learning Strategies

Resources: Locate several books about friends and friendship.

Directions

Step I: Have students brainstorm a list of adjectives that describe a good friend. Remember that all contributions are acceptable.

Step II: Working in small groups, students should read three or more books that tell about some good friends, the problems they have, and how they solved them. The group should discuss the following questions:
1. Why do we need friends?
2. How are friends different from relatives or members of the family?
3. Are some friends better than others?

Step III: Have each student write an essay on the topic "What Friendship Means to Me."

Assessment Performance

1. Students will work in pairs to edit their essays.
2. The essays will be published in a class book titled *All About Friendship*.

Thinking + Lesson Plan 9. *Teaching With Picture Books in the Middle School* by Iris McClellan Tiedt, ©2000 International Reading Association. May be copied.

Thinking + Lesson Plan 10
Title of Lesson: Understanding Stereotyped Thinking

Expected Outcomes

The learner will

1. list words that describe the wolf.
2. read fiction and nonfiction about wolves.
3. compare their thinking about wolves before and after this study.
4. compose statements about stereotyped thinking.

Teaching/Learning Strategies

Resources: Locate several picture books about wolves.

Directions

Step I: Ask students to brainstorm words that describe a wolf. Write these words on the board as they are suggested.

Step II: Then have each student compose a summary sentence about a wolf, for example: *A wolf is a ferocious animal that kills sheep.* Have students save these sentences in their journals.

Step III: Divide students into groups of three to five students each. Give each group one or two picture books that deal with wolves. Include at least one fictional story about a wolf. Group members should take turns reading the books aloud.

Step IV: After students read the books aloud, have each group discuss the images of the wolf presented in each book.

Step V: Then have each student read his or her summary sentence aloud and decide if that sentence needs to be changed in any way. Students can then revise their sentences to use as the topic sentence for a paragraph about wolves.

Step VI: Discuss with the class the stereotyped thinking many people have about wolves. Guide them to construct a generalization about stereotyped thinking.

Assessment Performance

Students will identify examples of stereotyped thinking when they occur in literature or in behaviors they observe.

Thinking + Lesson Plan 11
Title of Lesson: Building Walls

Expected Outcomes

The learner will

1. discuss the topic of walls.
2. learn about specific walls around the world.
3. make a presentation and write poetry.

Teaching/Learning Strategies

Resources: Obtain a copy of *Talking Walls* by Margy B. Knight; locate a copy of Robert Frost's poem "Mending Wall."

Directions

Step I: Read the poem "Mending Wall" aloud to the class. Display the following lines from the poem on a transparency or a poster:

> Before I built a wall I'd ask to know
> What I was walling in or walling out....

Discuss the kinds of walls students know about and what walls achieve.

Step II: Give students working in small groups a specific wall to investigate using those in Knight's book or others you know. Students should engage in library and Internet research.

Step III: Each group will deliver a presentation about their wall.

Step IV: Ask students to discuss the effect of walls and to write poems to express their ideas.

Assessment Performance

1. Students will publish their poems in a class book titled *If Walls Could Talk*.
2. Students will share their presentations with parents and another class.

Thinking + Lesson Plan 12
Title of Lesson: Evaluating the Art in Picture Books

Expected Outcomes

The learner will

1. read a number of picture books.
2. use a set of criteria to evaluate the art in these books.

Teaching/Learning Strategy

Resources: An assortment of picture books that feature attractive art that students can admire, evaluate, and perhaps emulate.

Directions

Give each pair of students two picture books to examine. The focus is on the art, but students also will be interested in the story or information presented.

Step I: Tell students to study the art in the books they have. Ask them to identify the artist, reading information supplied about the person and the type of art selected for this book.

Step II: Then ask the class to begin compiling a list of the qualities that make art particularly outstanding in a picture book. List these on the chalkboard as students make individual contributions. Discuss the qualities, eliminating duplicates and modifying others as necessary. Have a student enter the list, which forms a kind of rubric, on the computer, printing about six copies.

Step III: During the following class divide the class into groups of four or five students, and give each group three or four picture books to evaluate. The group is to examine each book and to rank it 5 (very good), 3 (ok), or 1 (not acceptable) for each item on the list of qualities identified. They should then add the total for each book, giving the book a numerical score that can be compared to the score received by other books. Display the several books that receive the highest scores and discuss why they seem outstanding.

Assessment Performance

Give each student a book to evaluate using the same criteria as that used by the group in the class activity. Have each student present the book and his or her evaluation to a small group.

Thinking + Lesson Plan 13
Title of Lesson: Creating a Mural With Marbleized Paper

Expected Outcomes

The learner will

1. examine the art techniques used by one illustrator.
2. create marbleized paper.
3. use the paper to make figures that represent our diverse population.
4. share in making a class mural that conveys a message to other students.

Teaching/Learning Strategy

Resources: Obtain several copies of *The Snowy Day* by Ezra Jack Keats, which won the Caldecott Award. Also, try to locate the film about this author/illustrator by Weston Woods in which he describes exactly how to produce the paper he uses in the illustrations in this book. Collect the art supplies underlined in the following procedure.

Directions

Step I: Show the film and then read the story aloud, showing the illustrations as you go. Pass around copies of the book so students can examine the marbleized paper art more closely.

Step II: Set up stations at which students can take turns creating marbleized paper. Float drops of enamel paint on water in large shallow pans. Lay a 12″ × 18″ sheet of paper gently over the water to pick up the swirls of paint. Lift the sheet and place it on the floor to dry. Experiment with colors and designs.

Step III: Study picture books for ideas for different kinds of clothing. Have students cut out clothing shapes from the marbleized paper plus heads, hands, and feet cut from other paper of various flesh tones to create people. Students can share the different papers. They glue the figures marching in a parade on a large sheet of paper to create a class mural with the title "We Live in a Multiculture." Students can paint background plants, trees, and buildings to complete the mural.

Assessment Performance

1. Display the mural in the school hall or library where it can be admired by other students in the school.
2. Have students discuss the message they are sharing through their art. Have them decide if they want to follow up this effort with other activities.

For books that will provide ideas about clothing representing different cultures, refer to Chapter 7.

Thinking + Lesson Plan 13. *Teaching With Picture Books in the Middle School* by Iris McClellan Tiedt, ©2000 International Reading Association. May be copied.

Thinking + Lesson Plan 14
Title of Lesson: Autobiographical Writing—Memories

Expected Outcomes

The learner will

1. write a short personal essay about childhood memories.
2. publish the story to share with the class and his or her family.

Teaching/Learning Strategy

Resources: Obtain a copy of *Spoken Memories* by Aliki. This story is presented with *Painted Words* in the same volume: *Marianthe's Story*. By turning over the book you will see that each story has its own front cover and title page. Together the stories tell readers how it feels to be an immigrant, leaving home and going to a new school where you don't understand the language.

Directions

Read *Spoken Memories* aloud. Discuss how Mari and her family must have felt as they left friends and relatives in their homeland, Greece, to go to a new country.

Step I: Have students divide into small groups. Each one can share a memory about saying good-bye to someone they care about. Some children may be immigrants; others may have moved.

Step II: Have each student make a list titled "Things I Remember From My Childhood."

Step III: Then have each student write an essay or story about his or her early years based on these memories.

Step IV: After sharing their writing with their classmates, students edit the stories and bind them in books to be given as a gift to their families.

Assessment Performance

1. Each student will share his or her story with the class.
2. Each student will produce a book.

Thinking + Lesson Plan 15
Title of Lesson: Quilting Stories

Expected Outcomes

The learner will

1. create a block to add to a class quilt.
2. write a paragraph or poem to display beside the quilt.

Teaching/Learning Strategy

Resources: Locate a copy of one of the books about quilts listed on page 131, for example: *Sweet Clara and the Freedom Quilt.*

Directions

Step I: In small groups, have students examine two to three books about quilts, discussing the importance quilts played in the lives of different families.

Step II: Have each student design a quilt square following any theme the class selects, such as friendship, peace, or memories.

Step III: Have each student write a poem or a paragraph about the ideas in his or her square.

Assessment Performance

1. The quilt will be assembled and displayed on the wall in the classroom or in the hallway near the school office.
2. Student writing will be displayed around the quilt.

Thinking + Lesson Plan 16
Title of Lesson: An Immigrant's Story

Expected Outcomes

The learner will

1. read a book about an immigrant's experience.
2. write a "point-of-view" story about an immigrant family.

Teaching/Learning Strategy

Resources: Obtain a copy of Harriet Ziefert's *When I First Came to This Land*.

Directions

Step I: Read *When I First Came to This Land* aloud to the class. Discuss how a person might feel about leaving the country in which he was born and arriving in a strange new land. Imagine how it would be not to know the language. Perhaps children in the class could share their experiences.

Step II: Working in cooperative learning groups, have students invent a scenario about a family who leaves a country currently in the news. Begin a story map on large sheets of paper on the floor as students list the characters, suggest possible settings, and begin imagining the events that might occur as they develop the plot.

Step III: Ask students to write a story together dictated line by line on a computer. Encourage them to take turns typing and to revise freely as different ideas come to mind. After saving their work, they can print several copies of a first draft to reread and edit in their group, as needed. Changes then can be made, and a final draft printed.

Step IV: Have each group share its story with the whole class. Students can vote on the best story to develop as a play to perform for another class.

Assessment Performance

1. Students will perform the play.
2. Students will write an evaluation of this learning activity in their learning logs, including what they learned as a result.

Thinking + Lesson Plan 17
Title: Different Kinds of Love

Expected Outcomes

The learner will

1. read Shel Silverstein's *The Giving Tree*.
2. discuss how we show love for other people.
3. write a story or poem about a family member they love.

Teaching/Learning Strategies

Resources: Find a copy of Shel Silverstein's *The Giving Tree* and other books about loving relationships.

Directions

Step I: Read *The Giving Tree* aloud. Have students discuss the relationship between the tree and boy (who becomes a man).

Step II: Have students work in small groups to read another book in which a loving relationship is expressed, for example, *Three Cheers for Catherine the Great!*, written by Cari Best and illustrated by Giselle Potter.

Step III: Have students write a paragraph about the different kinds of love they observe in *The Giving Tree* and in the other books they read. They might comment on the importance of love to each of the characters they read about.

Assessment Performance

1. Students will share their writing in the small groups. Each group will select one student's writing to share with the whole class.
2. The class will agree on a concluding sentence or two about the kind of love that would have the most to offer them.

Exploring Further

The ideas presented in this book and the books suggested are enough to get you started with using exciting picture books to enhance your teaching in the middle school. In this appendix I list resources that will help you locate more information. Included, too, is a list of books that have won the Caldecott Award.

Resources for the Teacher

Selected Web sites

The Internet is an excellent source of up-to-date information. Following are a few addresses you might like to investigate. Also check out sites for your local library and bookstores.

The ALAN Review
scholar.lib.vt.edu/ejournals/ALAN/alan-review.html

American Library Association's *Booklist*
www.ala.org/booklist/index.html

The Horn Book
www.hbook.com

Bookwire
www.bookwire.com/

The Lion and the Unicorn
muse.jhu.edu/journals/uni

Professional Journals

You may want to subscribe to some of the following journals, which will help you update your knowledge about teaching and resources that are available to you. Titles marked with an asterisk come as part of membership in a professional organization that presents conferences and provides other support for teachers.

Book Links: Connecting Books, Libraries, and Classrooms. American Library Association, 50 Huron St., Chicago, IL 60611; www.ala.org/Booklinks Subscription; published bimonthly.

*English Journal. National Council of Teachers of English, 1111 W. Kenyon Rd., Urbana, IL 61801; www.ncte.org. Available with membership in NCTE; directed to middle and secondary school teachers.

*Journal of Adolescent & Adult Literacy. International Reading Association, 800 Barksdale Rd., Newark, Delaware 19714; www.reading.org. Available with membership in IRA; directed to middle school and secondary school teachers.

*Journal of Children's Literature. Children's Literature Assembly, National Council of Teachers of English, 1111 W. Kenyon Rd., Urbana, IL 61801; www.ncte.org. Available with membership in NCTE plus membership in the Assembly.

*Language Arts. National Council of Teachers of English, 1111 W. Kenyon Rd., Urbana, IL 61801; www.ncte.org. Available with membership in NCTE; directed to elementary and middle school teachers.

The New Advocate. Christopher-Gordon Publishers, Inc., 480 Washington St., Norwood, MA 02062. Published quarterly.

*The Reading Teacher. International Reading Association, 800 Barksdale Rd., Newark, DE 19714; www.reading.org. Available with membership in IRA; directed to elementary and middle school teachers.

Selected Articles in Professional Journals

Farris, P.J., & Fuhler, C.J. (1994). Developing social studies concepts through picture books. *The Reading Teacher, 47*, 380–387.

Morado, C., Koenig, R., & Wilson, A. (1999). Miniperformances, many stars! Playing with stories. *The Reading Teacher, 53*, 116–123.

Paley, V. (1999, May/June). K is for kindness. *Teacher Magazine*, pp. 40–42.

Tiedt, I.M. (1999, November/December). Introducing children to conservation. *Science and Children, 37*, 18–21.

Towell, J.H. (1999). Motivating students through music and literature. *The Reading Teacher, 53*, 284–86.

Walker, S.M. (1998, September). Wolves in fact and fiction. *Book Links, 8*, 17–20.

Professional Books

Allen, J. (Ed.). (1999). *Class actions: Teaching for social justice in elementary and middle school.* New York: Teachers College Press.

Beaty, J.J. (1997). *Building bridges with multicultural picture books.* Columbus, OH: Merrill.

Benedict, S., & Carlisle, L. (Eds.). (1992). *Beyond words: Picture books for older readers and writers.* Portsmouth, NH: Heinemann.

Blatt, G. (Ed.). (1993). *Once upon a folktale: Capturing the folklore process with children.* New York: Teacher's College Press.

Bosma, B., & Guth, N.D. (Eds.). (1995). *Children's literature in an integrated curriculum: The authentic voice.* New York: Teachers College Press; Newark, DE: International Reading Association.

Bromley, K.D. (1991). *Webbing with literature: Creating story maps with children's books.* Boston: Allyn and Bacon.

California Curriculum Development and Supplemental Materials Commission. (1999). *Reading/language arts framework for California public schools: Kindergarten through grade twelve.* Sacramento, CA: California Department of Education.

Committee to Revise the Multicultural Booklist. (1997). *Kaleidoscope: A multicultural booklist for grades K–8* (2nd ed.). Urbana, IL: National Council of Teachers of English.

Cooper, C.H. (1996). *ABC books and activities: From preschool to high school.* Lanham, MD: Scarecrow Press.

Finders, M.J. (1997). *Hidden literacies & life in junior high.* New York: Teachers College Press.

Forte, I., & Schurr, S. (1995). *Using favorite picture books to stimulate discussion and to encourage critical thinking.* Nashville, TN: Incentive Publishers.

Freeman, E., & Person, D. (Eds.). (1992). *Using nonfiction trade books in the elementary classroom: From ants to zeppelins.* Urbana, IL: National Council of Teachers of English.

Golub, J. (1994). *Activities for an interactive classroom.* Urbana, IL; National Council of Teachers of English.

Hall, S. (1994). *Using picture storybooks to teach literary devices.* Phoenix, AZ: Oryx Press.

Hart-Hewins, L., & Wells, J. (1990). *Real books for reading: Learning to read with children's literature.* Portsmouth, NH: Heinemann.

Hurd, P.D. (1999). *Transforming middle school science education.* New York: Teachers College Press.

International Reading Association & National Council of Teachers of English. (1996). *Standards for the English language arts.* Newark, DE: International Reading Association; Urbana, IL: National Council of Teachers of English.

Kiedfer, B. (1995). The potential of picturebooks: From visual literacy to aesthetic understanding. Englewood Cliffs, NJ: Prentice Hall.

Ladson-Billings, G. (1994). *The dreamkeepers: Successful teaching of African American children.* San Francisco: Jossey-Bass.

Lima C.W., & Lima, J.A. (1993). *A to zoo: Subject access to children's picture books.* Detroit, MI: Bowker.

McAllister, D. (1993). *Expanding the use of picture storybooks with older readers.* CRA Yearbook. Costa Mesa, CA: California Reading Association.

Middle Grade Task Force. (1987). *Caught in the middle: Educational reform for young adolescents in California public schools.* Los Angeles: California State Department of Education.

Newman, S. (1992). *Multicultural picture books: Art for understanding others* (Professional Growth Series). Orthington, OH: Linworth.

Nicholson-Nelson, K. (1998). *Developing multiple intelligences.* New York: Scholastic.

O'Sullivan, C. (1994). *The challenge of picture books: A teacher's guide to the use of picture books with older students.* New York: Teachers College Press.

Pella, M.L. (1987). *Resources for middle-grade reluctant readers: A guide for librarians.* Englewood, CA: Libraries Unlimited.

Phelan, P. (Ed.). (1989). *Talking to learn.* Urbana, IL: National Council of Teachers of English.

Rief, L. (1992). *Seeking diversity: Language arts with adolescents.* Portsmouth, NH: Heinemann.

Schiro, M. (1997). *Integrating children's literature and mathematics in the classroom.* New York: Teachers College Press.

Simmons, J.S., & Baines, L. (Eds.). (1998). *Language study in middle school, high school, and beyond.* Newark, DE: International Reading Association.

Sorensen, M., & Lehman, B. (Eds.). (1995). *Teaching with children's books: Paths to literature-based instruction.* Urbana, IL: National Council of Teachers of English.

Soter, A.O. (1999). *Young adult literatue and the new literary theories.* New York: Teachers College Press.

Stewig, J. (1994). *Looking at picture books.* Fort Atkinson, WI: Highsmith.

Taylor, B.M., Graves, M.F., & van den Broek, P. (Eds.). (1999). *Reading for meaning: Fostering comprehension in the middle grades.* New York: Teachers College Press; Newark, DE: International Reading Association.

Tiedt, I. (1987). *The language arts handbook.* Englewood Cliffs, NJ: Prentice Hall.

Tiedt, I. (1989). *Exploring books with children.* Boston: Houghton Mifflin.

Tiedt, I. (1989). *Writing: From topic to evaluation.* Boston: Allyn & Bacon.

Tiedt, I.M., Carlson, J., Howard, B., & Watanabe, K. (1989). *Teaching thinking in K–12 classrooms: Ideas, activities, and resources.* Boston: Allyn & Bacon.

Tiedt, I.M., Gibbs, R., Howard, M., Timpson, M., & Williams, M. (1989). *Reading/ thinking/writing: A holistic language and literacy program for the K–8 classroom.* Boston: Allyn & Bacon.

Tiedt, P., & Tiedt, I.M. (1999). *Multicultural teaching: Ideas, activities, and resources* (5th ed.). Boston: Allyn & Bacon.

Wood, C. (1994). *Yardsticks: Children in the classroom, ages 4–12.* New York: Northeast Foundation for Children.

Additional Professional Resources

The International Reading Association and the Children's Book Council publish an annual list of picture books chosen by children as favorites titled *Children's Choices*. This list appears in the October issue of *The Reading Teacher*.

The International Reading Association also publishes a list of teachers' favorite books each year, *Teachers' Choices*, which appears in the November issue of *The Reading Teacher*.

Choices lists are also available from www.reading.org/choices.

The International Reading Association's Special Interest Group for Children's Literature and Reading publishes an annual list of multicultural trade books, *Notable Books for a Global Society*. See www.csulb.edu/org/childrens-lit/notable.html for ordering information.

Caldecott Award

Books and Honor Books

The following picture books have won the Randolph J. Caldecott Award given annually by the American Library Association. These books are recognized for their outstanding illustrations. In this list the artist who won the award is listed following the title of the book. At times the artist also wrote the book; if not, the author is indicated following the artist. The publisher is included in parentheses. Although all books listed did win awards, you will need to examine each title to see what it has to offer you and your class. Many of these books are recommended for specific uses throughout *Teaching With Picture Books in the Middle School*.

1938

Animals of the Bible: A Picture Book, illustrated by Dorothy P. Lathrop; text by Helen Dean Fish. (Lippincott)

Honor Books

Seven Simeons, retold and illustrated by Boris Artzybasheff. (Viking)

Four and Twenty Blackbirds, illustrated by Robert Lawson; text by Helen Dean Fish. (Stokes)

1939

Mei Li by Thomas Handforth. (Doubleday)

Honor Books

The Forest Pool by Laura Adams Armer. (Longmans)

Wee Gillis illustrated by Robert Lawson; text by Munro Leaf. (Viking)

Snow White and the Seven Dwarfs by Wanda Gag. (Coward)

Barkis by Clare Turlay Newberry. (Harper)

1940

Abraham Lincoln by Ingri and Edgar d'Aulaire. (Doubleday)

Honor Books

Cock-a-Doodle Doo by Berta and Elmer Hader. (Macmillan)

Madeline by Ludwig Bemelmans. (Viking)

The Ageless Story by Lauren Ford. (Dodd, Mead)

1941

They Were Strong and Good by Robert Lawson. (Viking)

Honor Book

April's Kittens by Clare Turlay Newberry. (Harper & Row)

1942

Make Way for Ducklings by Robert McCloskey. (Viking)

Honor Books

An American ABC by Maud and Miska Petersham. (Macmillan)
In My Mother's House, illustrated by Velino Herrera; text by Ann Nolan Clark. (Viking)
Paddle-to-the-Sea by Holling C. Holling. (Houghton Mifflin)
Nothing at All by Wanda Gag. (Coward)

1943

The Little House by Virginia Lee Burton. (Houghton Mifflin)

Honor Books

Dash and Dart by Mary and Conrad Buff. (Viking)
Marshmallow by Clare Turlay Newberry. (Harper & Row)

1944

Many Moons, illustrated by Louis Slobodkin; text by James Thurber. (Harcourt)

Honor Books

Small Rain: Verses From the Bible, illustrated by Elizabeth Orton Jones; selected by Jessie Orton Jones. (Viking)
Pierre Pigeon, illustrated by Arnold E. Bare; text by Lee Kingman. (Houghton Mifflin)
The Mighty Hunter by Berta and Elmer Hader. (Macmillan)
A Child's Good Night Book, illustrated by Jean Charlot; text by Margaret Wise Brown. (Scott)
Good Luck Horse, illustrated by Piao Chan; text by Chin-Yi Chan. (Whittlesey)

1945

Prayer for a Child, illustrated by Elizabeth Orton Jones; text by Rachel Field. (Macmillan)

Honor Books

Mother Goose by Tasha Tudor. (Walck)
In the Forest by Marie Hall Ets. (Viking)
Yonie Wondernose by Marguerite de Angeli. (Doubleday)
The Christmas Angel illustrated by Kate Seredy; text by Ruth Sawyer. (Viking)

1946

The Rooster Crows by Maud and Miska Petersham. (Macmillan)

Honor Books

Little Lost Lamb, illustrated by Leonard Weisgard; text by Golden MacDonald. (Doubleday)
Sing Mother Goose, illustrated by Marjorie Torrey; text by Opal Wheeler. (Dutton)
My Mother Is the Most Beautiful Woman in the World, illustrated by Ruth Gannett; text by Becky Reyher. (Lothrop)
You Can Write Chinese by Kurt Wiese. (Viking)

1947

The Little Island, illustrated by Leonard Weisgard; text by Golden MacDonald. (Doubleday)

Honor Books

Rain Drop Splash, illustrated by Leonard Weisgard; text by Alvin Tresselt. (Lothrop)
Boats on the River, illustrated by Jay Hyde Barnum; text by Marjorie Flack. (Viking)
Timothy Turtle, illustrated by Tony Palazzo; text by Al Graham. (Welch)
Pedro, The Angel of Olvera Street by Leo Politi. (Scribner)
Sing in Praise: A Collection of the Best Loved Hymns, illustrated by Marjorie Torrey; text selected by Opal Wheeler. (Dutton)

1948

White Snow, Bright Snow, illustrated by Roger Duviosin; text by Alvin Tresselt. (Lothrop)

Honor Books

Stone Soup by Marcia Brown. (Scribner)

McElligot's Pool by Dr. Seuss. (Random House)

Bambino the Clown by Georges Schreiber. (Viking)

Roger and the Fox, illustrated by Hildegard Woodward; text by Lavinia R. Davis. (Doubleday)

Song of Robin Hood, illustrated by Virginia Lee Burton; text edited by Anne Malcolmson. (Houghton)

1949

The Big Snow by Berta & Elmer Hader. (Macmillan)

Honor Books

Blueberries for Sal by Robert McCloskey. (Viking)

All Around The Town, illustrated by Helen Stone; text by Phyllis McGinley. (Lippincott)

Juanita by Leo Politi. (Scribner)

Fish in The Air by Kurt Wiese. (Viking)

1950

Song of The Swallows by Leo Politi (Scribner)

Honor Books

America's Ethan Allen, illustrated by Lynd Ward; text by Stewart Holbrook. (Houghton)

The Wild Birthday Cake, illustrated by Hildegard Woodward; text by Lavinia R. Davis. (Doubleday)

The Happy Day, illustrated by Marc Simont; text by Ruth Krauss. (Harper)

Bartholomew and The Oobleck by Dr. Seuss. (Random House)

Henry Fisherman by Marcia Brown

1951

The Egg Tree by Katherine Milhous. (Scribner)

Honor Books

Dick Whittington and His Cat by Marcia Brown. (Scribner)

The Two Reds, illustrated by Nicholas Mordvinoff; text by William Lipkind. (Harcourt)

If I Ran The Zoo by Dr. Seuss. (Random House)

The Most Wonderful Doll in The World, illustrated by Helen Stone; text by Phyllis McGinley. (Lippincott)

T-Bone, The Baby Sitter by Clare Turlay Newberry. (Harper)

1952

Finders Keepers, illustrated by Nicholas Mordvinoff; text by William Lipkind. (Harcourt)

Honor Books

Mr. T.W. Anthony Woo by Marie Hall Ets. (Viking)

Skipper John's Cook by Marcia Brown. (Scribner)

All Falling Down, illustrated by Margaret Bloy; text by Gene Zion. (Harper)

Bear Party by William Pène du Bois. (Viking)

Feather Mountain by Elizabeth Olds. (Houghton)

1953

The Biggest Bear by Lynd Ward. (Houghton)

Honor Books

Puss in Boots, illustrated by Marcia Brown; text translated from Charles Perrault by Marcia Brown. (Scribner)

One Morning in Maine by Robert McCloskey. (Viking)

Ape in a Cape: An Alphabet of Odd Animals by Fritz Eichenberg. (Harcourt)

The Storm Book, illustrated by Margaret Bloy Graham; text by Charlotte Zolotow. (Harper)

Five Little Monkeys by Juliet Kepes. (Houghton)

1954

Madeline's Rescue by Ludwig Bemelmans. (Viking)

Honor Books

Journey Cake, Ho!, illustrated by Robert McCloskey; text by Ruth Sawyer. (Viking)

When Will The World Be Mine?, illustrated by Jean Charlot; text by Miriam Schlein (W.R. Scott)

The Steadfast Tin Soldier, illustrated by Marcia Brown; text by Hans Christian Andersen, translated by M.R. James. (Scribner)

A Very Special House, illustrated by Maurice Sendak; text by Ruth Krauss. (Harper)

Green Eyes by A. Birnbaum. (Capitol)

1955

Cinderella: Or the Little Glass Slipper, illustrated by Marcia Brown; text translated from Charles Perrault by Marcia Brown. (Scribner)

Honor Books

Book of Nursery and Mother Goose Rhymes, illustrated by Marguerite de Angeli. (Doubleday)

Wheel On The Chimney, illustrated by Tibor Gergely; text by Margaret Wise Brown. (Lippincott)

The Thanksgiving Story, illustrated by Helen Sewell; text by Alice Dalgliesh. (Scribner)

1956

Frog Went A-Courtin', illustrated by Feodor Rojankovsky; text retold by John Langstaff. (Harcourt)

Honor Books

Play With Me by Marie Hall Ets. (Viking)

Crow Boy by Taro Yashima. (Viking)

1957

A Tree Is Nice, illustrated by Marc Simont; text by Janice Udry. (Harper)

Honor Books

Mr. Penny's Race Horse by Marie Hall Ets. (Viking)

1 Is One by Tasha Tudor. (Walck)

Anatole illustrated by Paul Galdone; text by Eve Titus. (McGraw-Hill)

Gillespie and the Guards, illustrated by James Daugherty; text by Benjamin Elkin. (Viking)

Lion by William Pène du Bois. (Viking)

1958

Time of Wonder by Robert McCloskey. (Viking)

Honor Books

Fly High, Fly Low by Don Freeman. (Viking)

Anatole and the Cat, illustrated by Paul Galdone; text by Eve Titus. (McGraw-Hill)

1959

Chanticleer and the Fox, illustrated by Barbara Cooney; text adapted from Chaucer's *Canterbury Tales* by Barbara Cooney. (Crowell)

Honor Books

The House that Jack Built: La Maison Que Jacques A Batie by Antonio Frasconi. (Harcourt)
What Do You Say, Dear?, illustrated by Maurice Sendak; text by Sesyle Joslin. (W.R. Scott)

1960

Nine Days to Christmas, illustrated by Marie Hall Ets; text by Marie Hall Ets and Aurora Labastida. (Viking)

Honor Books

Houses from the Sea, illustrated by Adrienne Adams; text by Alice E. Goudey. (Scribner)
The Moon Jumpers, illustrated by Maurice Sendak; text by Janice May Udry. (Harper)

1961

Baboushka and the Three Kings, illustrated by Nicolas Sidjakov; text by Ruth Robbins. (Parnassus)

Honor Book

Inch by Inch by Leo Lionni. (Obolensky)

1962

Once a Mouse, retold and illustrated by Marcia Brown. (Scribner)

Honor Books

Fox Went out on a Chilly Night: An Old Song by Peter Spier. (Doubleday)
Little Bear's Visit, illustrated by Maurice Sendak; text by Else H. Minarik. (Harper)
The Day We Saw the Sun Come Up, illustrated by Adrienne Adams; text by Alice E. Goudey. (Scribner)

1963

The Snowy Day by Ezra Jack Keats. (Viking)

Honor Books

The Sun Is a Golden Earring, illustrated by Bernarda Bryson; text by Natalia M. Belting. (Holt)

Mr. Rabbit and the Lovely Present, illustrated by Maurice Sendak; text by Charlotte Zolotow (Harper)

1964

Where the Wild Things Are by Maurice Sendak. (Harper)

Honor Books

Swimmy by Leo Lionni. (Pantheon)

All in the Morning Early, illustrated by Evaline Ness; text by Sorche Nic Leodhas. (Holt)

Mother Goose and Nursery Rhymes, illustrated by Philip Reed. (Atheneum)

1965

May I Bring a Friend?, illustrated by Beni Montresor; text by Beatrice Schenk de Regniers. (Atheneum)

Honor Books

Rain Makes Applesauce, illustrated by Marvin Bileck; text by Julian Scheer. (Holiday)

The Wave illustrated by Blair Lent; text by Margaret Hodges. (Houghton)

A Pocketful of Cricket, illustrated by Evaline Ness; text by Rebecca Caudill. (Holt)

1966

Always Room for One More, illustrated by Nonny Hogrogian; text by Sorche Nic Leodhas. (Holt)

Honor Books

Hide and Seek Fog, illustrated by Roger Duvoisin; text by Alvin Tresselt. (Lothrop)

Just Me by Marie Hall Ets. (Viking)

Tom Tit Tot, retold and illustrated by Evaline Ness. (Scribner)

1967

Sam, Bangs & Moonshine by Evaline Ness. (Holt)

Honor Book

One Wild River to Cross, illustrated by Ed Emberley; text adapted by Barbara Emerley. (Prentice Hall)

1968

Drummer Hoff, illustrated by Ed Emberley; text adapted by Barbara Emberley. (Prentice Hall)

Honor Books

Frederick by Leo Lionni. (Pantheon)
Seashore Story by Taro Yashima. (Viking)
The Emperor and the Kite, illustrated by Ed Young; text by Jane Yolen. (World)

1969

The Fool of the World and the Flying Ship, illustrated by Uri Shulevitz; text retold by Arthur Ransome. (Farrar)

Honor Book

Why the Sun and the Moon Live in the Sky, illustrated by Blair Lent; text by Elphinstone Dayrell. (Houghton)

1970

Sylvester and the Magic Pebble by William Steig. (Windmill Books)

Honor Books

Goggles! by Ezra Jack Keats. (Macmillian)
Alexander and the Wind-Up Mouse by Leo Lionni. (Pantheon)
Pop Corn & Ma Goodness, illustrated by Robert Andrew Parker; text by Edna Mitchell Preston. (Viking)
Thy Friend, Obadiah by Brinton Turkle. (Viking)
The Judge: An Untrue Tale, illustrated by Margot Zemach; text by Harve Zemach. (Farrar)

1971

A Story, a Story: An African Tale, retold and illustrated by Gail E. Haley. (Atheneum)

Honor Books

The Angry Moon, illustrated by Blair Lent; text retold by William Sleator. (Atlantic)

Frog and Toad Are Friends by Arnold Lobel. (Harper)

In the Night Kitchen by Maurice Sendak. (Harper)

1972

One Fine Day, retold and illustrated by Nonny Hogrogian. (Macmillian)

Honor Books

Hildilid's Night, illustrated by Arnold Lobel; text by Cheli Durán Ryan (Macmillian)

If All the Seas Were One Sea by Janina Domanska. (Macmillian)

Moja Means One: Swahili Counting Book, illustrated by Tom Feelings; text by Muriel Feelings. (Dial)

1973

The Funny Little Woman, illustrated by Blair Lent; text retold by Arlene Mosel. (Dutton)

Honor Books

Anansi the Spider: A Tale from the Ashanti, adapted and illustrated by Gerald McDermott (Holt)

Hosie's Alphabet, illustrated by Leonard Baskin; text by Hosea, Tobis, and Lisa Baskin. (Viking)

Snow-White and the Seven Dwarfs, illustrated by Nancy Ekholm Burkert; text translated by Randall Jerrell, retold from the Brothers Grimm. (Farrar)

When Clay Sings, illustrated by Tom Bahti; text by Byrd Baylor. (Scribner)

1974

Duffy and the Devil, illustrated by Margot Zemach; text retold by Harve Zemach. (Farrar)

Honor Books

Three Jovial Huntsmen by Susan Jeffers. (Bradbury)

Cathedral by David Macaulay. (Houghton)

1975

Arrow to the Sun by Gerald McDermott. (Viking)

Honor Book

Jambo Means Hello: A Swahili Alphabet Book, illustrated by Tom Feelings; text by Muriel Feelings. (Dial)

1976

Why Mosquitoes Buzz in People's Ears, illustrated by Leo & Diane Dillon; text retold by Verna Aardema. (Dial)

Honor Books

The Desert is Theirs, illustrated by Peter Parnall; text by Byrd Baylor. (Scribner)
Strega Nona by Tomie dePaola. (Prentice Hall)

1977

Ashanti to Zulu: African Traditions, illustrated by Leo & Diane Dillion; text by Margaret Musgrove. (Dial)

Honor Books

The Amazing Bone by William Steig. (Farrar)
The Contest, retold and illustrated by Nonny Hogrogian. (Greenwillow)
Fish for Supper by M.B. Goffstein. (Dial)
The Golem: A Jewish Legend by Beverly Brodsky McDermott. (Lippincott)
Hawk, I'm Your Brother, illustrated by Peter Parnall; text by Byrd Baylor. (Scribner)

1978

Noah's Ark by Peter Spier. (Doubleday)

Honor Books

Castle by David Macaulay. (Houghton)
It Could Always Be Worse, retold and illustrated by Margot Zemach. (Farrar)

1979

The Girl Who Loved Wild Horses by Paul Goble. (Bradbury)

Honor Books

Freight Train by Donald Crews. (Greenwillow)

The Way to Start a Day, illustrated by Peter Parnall; text by Byrd Baylor. (Scribner)

1980

Ox-Cart Man, illustrated by Barbara Cooney; text by Donald Hall. (Viking)

Honor Books

Ben's Trumpet by Rachel Isadora. (Greenwillow)

The Garden of Abdul Gasazi by Chris Van Allsburg. (Houghton)

The Treasure by Uri Shulevitz. (Farrar)

1981

Fables by Arnold Lobel. (Harper)

Honor Books

The Bremen-Town Musicians, retold and illustrated by Ilse Plume. (Doubleday)

The Grey Lady and the Strawberry Snatcher by Molly Bang. (Four Winds)

Mice Twice by Joseph Low. (McElderry/Atheneum)

Truck by Donald Crews. (Greenwillow)

1982

Jumanji by Chris Van Allsburg. (Houghton)

Honor Books

Where the Buffaloes Begin, illustrated by Stephen Gammell; text by Olaf Baker. (Warne)

On Market Street, illustrated by Anita Lobel; text by Arnold Lobel. (Greenwillow)

Outside Over There by Maurice Sendak. (Harper)

A Visit to William Blake's Inn: Poems for Innocent and Experience Travelers, illustrated by Alice & Martin Provensen; text by Nancy Willard. (Harcourt)

1983

Shadow, translated and illustrated by Marcia Brown; original text in French by Blaise Cendrars. (Scribner)

Honor Books

A Chair for My Mother by Vera B. Williams. (Greenwillow)
When I Was Young in the Mountains, illustrated by Diane Goode; text by Cynthia Rylant. (Dutton)

1984

The Glorious Flight: Across the Channel with Louis Bleriot by Alice & Martin Provensen. (Viking)

Honor Books

Little Red Riding Hood, retold and illustrated by Trina Schart Hyman. (Holiday)
Ten, Nine, Eight by Molly Bang. (Greenwillow)

1985

Saint George and the Dragon, illustrated by Trina Schart Hyman; text retold by Margaret Hodges. (Little, Brown)

Honor Books

Hansel and Gretel, illustrated by Paul O. Zelinsky; text retold by Rika Lesser. (Dodd)
Have You Seen My Duckling? by Nancy Tafuri. (Greenwillow)
The Story of Jumping Mouse: A Native American Legend, retold and illustrated by John Steptoe. (Lothrop)

1986

The Polar Express by Chris Van Allsburg. (Houghton)

Honor Books

The Relatives Came, illustrated by Stephen Gammell; text by Cynthia Rylant. (Bradbury)
King Bidgood's in the Bathtub, illustrated by Don Wood; text by Audrey Wood. (Harcourt)

1987

Hey, Al, illustrated by Richard Egielski; text by Arthur Yorinks. (Philomel)

Honor Books

The Village of Round and Square Houses by Ann Grifalconi. (Little, Brown)
Alphabatics by Suse MacDonald. (Bradbury)
Rumpelstiltskin by Paul O. Zelinsky. (Dutton)

1988

Owl Moon, illustrated by John Schoenherr; text by Jane Yolen. (Philomel)

Honor Book

Mufaro's Beautiful Daughters: An African Tale by John Steptoe. (Lothrop)

1989

Song and Dance Man, illustrated by Stephen Gammell; text by Karen Ackerman. (Knopf)

Honor Books

The Boy of the Three-Year Nap, illustrated by Allen Say; text by Diane Snyder. (Houghton)
Free Fall by David Wiesner. (Lothrop)
Goldilocks and the Three Bears by James Marshall. (Dial)
Mirandy and Brother Wind, illustrated by Jerry Pinkney; text by Patricia C. McKissack. (Knopf)

1990

Lon Po Po: A Red-Riding Hood Story From China by Ed Young. (Philomel)

Honor Books

Bill Peet: An Autobiography by Bill Peet. (Houghton)
Color Zoo by Lois Ehlert. (Lippincott)
The Talking Eggs: A Folktale from the American South, illustrated by Jerry Pinkney; text by Robert D. San Souci. (Dial)
Hershel and the Hanukkah Goblins, illustrated by Trina Schart Hyman; text by Eric Kimmel. (Holiday)

1991

Black and White by David Macaulay. (Hougthon)

Honor Books

Puss in Boots, illustrated by Fred Marcellino; text by Charles Perrault, translated by Malcolm Arthur. (DiCapua/Farrar)

"More, More, More," said the Baby: Three Love Stories by Vera B. Williams. (Greenwillow)

1992

Tuesday by David Wiesner. (Clarion)

Honor Book

Tar Beach by Faith Ringgold. (Crown)

1993

Mirette on the High Wire by Emily Arnold McCully. (Putnam)

Honor Books

The Stinky Cheese Man and Other Fairly Stupid Tales, illustrated by Lane Smith; text by Jon Scieszka. (Viking)

Seven Blind Mice by Ed Young. (Philomel)

Working Cotton, illustrated by Carole Byard; text by Sherley Anne Williams. (Harcourt)

1994

Grandfather's Journey, illustrated by Allen Say; text by Eve Bunting. (Harcourt)

Honor Books

Peppe the Lamplighter, illustrated by Ted Lewin; text by Elisa Bartone. (Lothrop)

In the Small, Small Pond by Denise Fleming. (Holt)

Raven: A Trickster Tale from the Pacific Northwest by Gerald McDermott. (Harcourt)

Owen by Kevin Henkes. (Greenwillow)

Yo! Yes?, illustrated by Chris Raschka; text edited by Richard Jackson. (Orchard)

1995

Smoky Night, illustrated by David Diaz; text by Eve Bunting. (Harcourt)

Honor Books

John Henry, illustrated by Jerry Pinkney; text by Julius Lester. (Dial)
Swamp Angel, illustrated by Paul O. Zelinsky; text by Anne Issacs. (Dutton)
Time Flies by Eric Rohmann. (Crown)

1996

Officer Buckle and Gloria by Peggy Rathmann. (Putnam)

Honor Books

Alphabet City by Stephen T. Johnson. (Viking)
Zin! Zin! Zin! a Violin, illustrated by Marjorie Priceman; text by Lloyd Moss. (Simon & Schuster)
The Faithful Friend, illustrated by Brian Pinkney; text by Robert D. San Souci. (Simon & Schuster)
Tops & Bottoms, adapted and illustrated by Janet Stevens. (Harcourt)

1997

Golem by David Wisniewski. (Clarion)

Honor Books

Hush! A Thai Lullaby, illustrated by Holly Meade; text by Minfong Ho. (Melanie Kroupa/Orchard Books)
The Graphic Alphabet by David Pelletier. (Orchard Books)
The Paperboy by Dav Pilkey. (Richard Jackson/Orchard Books)
Starry Messenger by Peter Sís. (Frances Foster Books/Farrar, Straus & Giroux)

1998

Rapunzel by Paul O. Zelinsky. (Dutton)

Honor Books

The Gardner, illustrated by David Small; text by Sarah Stewart. (Farrar)
Harlem, illustrated by Christopher Myers; text by Walter Dean Myers. (Scholastic)
There Was an Old Lady Who Swallowed a Fly by Simms Taback. (Viking)

1999

Snowflake Bentley, illustrated by Mary Azarian; text by Jacqueline Briggs Martin. (Houghton)

Honor Books

Duke Ellington: The Piano and the Orchestra, illustrated by Brian Pinkney; text by Andrea Davis Pinkney. (Hyperion)

No, David! by David Shannon. (Scholastic)

Snow by Uri Shulevitz. (Farrar)

Tibet Through the Red Box by Peter Sìs. (Frances Foster)

2000

Joseph Has a Little Overcoat by Simms Taback. (Viking)

Honor Books

A Child's Calendar, illustrated by Trina Schart Hyman; text by John Updike. (Holiday House)

Sector 7 by David Wiesner. (Clarion)

When Sophie Gets Angry—Really, Really Angry by Molly Bang. (Scholastic)

The Ugly Duckling, illustrated by Jerry Pinkney; from Hans Christian Andersen, adapted by Jerry Pinkney. (Morrow)

REFERENCES

Macrorie, K. (1994). *Searching writing*. Westport, CT: Greenwood.

Tiedt, I. (1999). Introducing conservation to children. *Science and Children, 37*, 18–21

Tiedt, P., & Tiedt, I. (1999). *Multicultural teaching* (5th ed.). Boston: Allyn & Bacon.

Tiedt, P., Tiedt, I., & Tiedt, S. (2000). *Language arts activities for the classroom* (3rd ed.). Boston: Allyn & Bacon.

Children's Literature References

Chapter 1

Aardema, V. (1976). *Why mosquitoes buzz in people's ears*. New York: Dial.

Angelou, M. (1987). *Now Sheba sings the song*. New York: Dutton/Dial.

Bemelmans, L. (1939). *Madeline*. New York: Viking.

Budd, J. (1995). *Horses: History, behavior, breeds, riding, jumping*. New York: Kingfisher.

Collay, R., & Dubrow, J. (1998). *Stuartship*. Eugene, OR: FlowerPress.

De Brunhoff, J. (1933). *The story of Babar, the little elephant*. New York: Random House.

Goble, P. (1978). *The girl who loved wild horses*. New York: Bradbury.

Gwynne, F. (1976). *A chocolate moose for dinner*. Englewood Cliffs, NJ: Prentice Hall.

Hodges, M. (1965). *The wave*. New York: Holiday House.

Keats, E.J. (1963). *The snowy day*. New York: Viking.

Knight, M.B. (1992). *Talking walls*. Gardiner, ME: Tilbury House.

Lewis, R. (Ed.). (1965). *In a spring garden*. New York: Dial.

Lyon, G.E. (1999). *Book*. New York: DK Publishing.

Mayer, M. (1974). *Frog, where are you?* New York: Dial.

McCloskey, R. (1941). *Make way for ducklings*. New York: Viking.

McDermott, G. (1974). *Arrow to the sun: A Pueblo Indian tale*. New York: Viking.

Ness, E. (1967). *Sam, bangs & moonshine*. New York: Holt.

Piper, W. (1954). *The little engine that could*. New York: Platt & Munk.

Ringgold, F. (1991). *Tar beach*. New York: Crown.

Rylant, C. (1982). *When I was young in the mountains*. New York: Dutton.

Sendak, M. (1963). *Where the wild things are*. New York: Harper.

Seuss, Dr. (1937). *And to think that I saw it on Mulberry Street*. New York: Vanguard.

Van Allsburg, C. (1984). *The mysteries of Harris Burdick*. Boston: Houghton Mifflin.

Yashima, T. (1955). *Crow boy*. New York: Viking.

Yolen, J. (1987). *Owl moon*. New York: Philomel.

Chapter 2

Arnold, T. (1990). *Mother Goose's words of wit and wisdom: A book of months*. New York: Dial.

Arnold, T. (1993). *The three billy goats gruff*. New York: Macmillan.

Aylesworth, J. (1998). *The gingerbread boy*. New York: Scholastic.

Browne, A. (1981). *Hansel and Gretel*. Danbury, CT: Watts.

Carle, E. (1988). *Eric Carle's treasury of classic stories for children*. Danbury, CT: Watts.

Denton, K.M. (1998). *A child's treasury of nursery rhymes*. New York: Kingfisher.

dePaola, T. (1985). *Tomie dePaola's Mother Goose*. New York: Putnam.

Edens, C. (1998). *The glorious Mother Goose*. New York: Atheneum.

Fabian, B. (1997). *Twinkle, twinkle: An animal lover's Mother Goose*. New York: Dutton.

Galdone, P. (1973). *The three billy goats gruff*. New York: Clarion.

Galdone, P. (1975). *The gingerbread boy*. Boston: Houghton Mifflin.

Goodall, J. (1988). *Little red riding hood*. New York: Margaret K. McElderry.

Grover, E.O. (1997). *Mother Goose: The original Volland edition*. New York: Checkerboard Press.

Hale, S.J. (1984). *Mary had a little lamb*. New York: Holiday House.

Hansel and Gretel, music by E. Humperdinck (various recordings).

Hobson, S. (1994). *Chicken little*. New York: Simon & Schuster.

Howe, J. (1989). *Jack and the beanstalk*. Boston: Little, Brown.

Hyman, T.S. (1983). *Little red riding hood*. New York: Holiday House.

Jeffers, S. (1980). *Hansel and Gretel*. New York: Dial

Lobel, A. (1986). *The Random House book of Mother Goose: A treasury of 306 timeless nursery rhymes*. New York: Random House.

Marshall, J. (1988). *Goldilocks and the three bears*. New York: Dial.

Montresor, B. (1991). *Little red riding hood*. New York: Doubleday.

Perrault, C. (1697). *Contes de Ma Mere L'Oye*.

Ray, J. (1997). *Hansel and Gretel*. Boston: Candlewick.

Voake, C. (1991). *The three little pigs and other favorite nursery stories*. Boston: Candlewick.

Wildsmith, B. (1964). *Brian Wildsmith's Mother Goose: A collection of nursery rhymes*. Danbury, CT: Watts.

Zimmerman, H.W. (1989). *Henny penny*. New York: Scholastic.

Chapter 3

Allard, H. (1977). *Miss Nelson is missing*. New York: Scholastic.

Andersen, H.C. (1998). *The emperor's new clothes: An all-star illustrated retelling of the classic fairy tale*. New York: Simon & Schuster (Audio).

Brett, J. (1994). *Town mouse and the country mouse.* New York: Putnam.

Buchanan, K. (1991). *This house is made of mud/Esta casa esta hecha de lodo.* Flagstaff, AZ: Northland.

Carle, E. (1971). *Do you want to be my friend?.* New York: HarperCollins.

Carr, J. (1999). *Swine divine.* New York: Holiday House.

De Brunhoff, J. (1933). *The story of Babar, the little elephant.* New York: Random House.

Denton, K.M. (1995). *Would they love a lion?* New York: Kingfisher.

Dorros, A. (1991). *Abuela.* New York: Dutton.

Ehlert, L. (1990). *Feathers for lunch.* San Diego, CA: Harcourt Brace.

Ehlert, L. (1998). *Top cat.* San Diego, CA: Harcourt Brace.

Estes, K.R. (1999). *Manuela's gift.* New York: Chronicle Books.

Feldman, J. (1991). *The alphabet in nature.* New York: Children's Book Press.

Feldman, J. (1992). *Shapes in nature.* New York: Children's Book Press.

Finchler, J. (1998). *Miss Malarkey won't be in today.* New York: Walker.

Glass, A. (1995). *Folks call me Appleseed John.* New York: Doubleday.

Gray, L.M. (1997). *Is there room on the feather bed?* New York: Orchard Books.

Hamilton, V. (1998). *In the beginning: Creation stories from around the world.* San Diego, CA: Harcourt Brace.

Harley, B. (1996). *Sarah's story.* Berkeley, CA: Tricycle Press.

Herman, G. (1996). *The littlest duckling.* New York: Viking.

Hest, A. (1986). *The purple coat.* New York: Simon & Schuster.

Hest, A. (1987). *Fancy Aunt Jess.* New York: Morrow Junior Books

Hest, A. (1993). *Nana's birthday party.* New York: Morrow.

Hoban, R. (1960). *Bedtime for Frances.* New York: Harper.

Hort, L. (1987). *The boy who held back the sea.* New York: Dial.

Huck, C. (1989). *Princess Furball.* New York: Greenwillow.

Isaacs, A. (1994). *Swamp angel.* New York: Dutton.

Jarrell, R. (1972). *Snow White and the seven dwarfs: A tale from the Brothers Grimm.* New York: Farrar, Straus & Giroux

Johnson, C. (1955). *Harold and the purple crayon.* New York: Harper.

Jordan, J. (1975). *New life: New room.* New York: Crowell.

Kipling, R. (1997). *Rikki Tikki Tavi.* New York: Morrow.

Krahn, F. (1968). *A flying saucer full of spaghetti.* New York: Delacorte.

Lester, J. (1994). *John Henry.* New York: Dial.

Lexau, J.M. (1965). *I should have stayed in bed.* New York: Harper.

Lobel, A. (1975). *Owl at home.* New York: Harper.

Lyon, G.E. (1999). *Book.* New York: DK Publishing.

Martin, B. Jr (1983). *Brown bear, brown bear, what do you see?* New York: Holt.

Mayer, M. (1967). *A boy, a dog, and a frog.* New York: Dial.

Mayer, M. (1973). *Frog on his own.* New York: Dial.

Mayer, M. (1974). *Frog goes to dinner.* New York: Dial

Mayer, M. (1974). *Frog, where are you?* New York: Dial.

Mayer, M. (1976). *A boy, a dog, a frog, and a friend.* New York: Dial.

McCully, E.A. (1992). *Mirette on the high wire.* New York: Putnam.

Miller, W. (1997). *Richard Wright and the library card.* New York: Lee & Low.

Milton, N. (1992). *The giraffe that walked to Paris.* New York: Crown.

Morozumi, A. (1998). *My friend gorilla.* New York: Farrar, Straus & Giroux.

Offen, H. (1996). *Nice work, little wolf!* New York: Dutton.

Parish, H. (1995). *Good driving, Amelia Bedelia.* New York: Greenwillow.

Parish, H. (1997). *Bravo, Amelia Bedelia!* New York: Morrow.

Parish, H. (1999). *Amelia 4 mayor.* New York: Greenwillow.

Pinkney, G.J. (1992). *Back home.* New York: Dial.

Ringgold, F. (1991). *Tar beach.* New York: Crown.

Rochelle, B. (1998). *Jewels.* New York: Lodestar.

Rohmann, E. (1994). *Time flies.* New York: Crown.

Sandburg, C. (1999). *The Huckabuck family and how they raised popcorn in Nebraska and quit and came back.* New York: Farrar, Straus & Giroux.

Seuss, Dr. (1938). *The 500 hats of Bartholomew Cubbins.* New York: Vanguard.

Seuss, Dr. (1947). *McElligott's pool.* New York: Random House.

Seuss, Dr. (1957). *The cat and the hat.* New York: Random House.

Simms, L. (1998). *Rotten teeth.* Boston: Houghton Mifflin.

Ungerer, T. (1967). *Moon man.* New York: Harper.

Van Allsburg, C. (1984). *The mysteries of Harris Burdick.* Boston: Houghton Mifflin.

Van Laan, N. (1998). *So say the little monkeys.* New York: Atheneum.

Waber, B. (1965). *Lyle, Lyle, crocodile.* Boston: Houghton Mifflin.

Waber, B. (1972). *Ira sleeps over.* Boston: Houghton Mifflin Audio.

Waite, J. (1998). *Mouse, look out!* New York: Dutton.

Weil, L. (1990). *Let's go to the library.* New York: Holiday House.

Wells, R. (1998). *Mary on horseback: Three mountain stories.* New York: Dial.

Williams, B. (1975). *Kevin's grandma.* New York: Dutton.

Williams, J. (1973). *Petronella.* Bowling Green, KY: Parents.

Wood, A. (1996). *The Bunyans.* New York: Scholastic.

Chapter 4

Adler, D.A. (1994). *A picture book of sojourner truth.* New York: Holiday House.

Ahlberg, J., & Ahlberg, A. (1986). *The jolly postman or other people's letters.* Boston: Little, Brown.

Atwood, A. (1973). *My own rhythm: An approach to haiku.* New York: Scribner.

Atwood, A. (1977). *Haiku: Vision in poetry and photography.* New York: Scribner.

Baylor, B. (1975). *The desert is theirs.* New York: Antheneum.

Baylor, B. (1977). *Everybody needs a rock.* New York: Scribner.

Baylor, B. (1986). *I'm in charge of celebrations.* New York: Antheneum.

Behn, H. (1964). *Cricket songs.* San Diego, CA: Harcourt Brace.

Benjamin, A.H. (1998). *It could have been worse.* Waukesha, WI: Little Tiger Press.

Bjork, C. (1987). *Linnea in Monet's garden.* New York: R & S Books.

Brill, M.T. (1998). *Diary of a drummer boy.* Brookfield, CT: Millbrook Press.

Bryan, A. (1993). *The story of lightning & thunder.* New York: Atheneum.

Budd, J. (1995). *Horses: History, behavior, breeds, riding, jumping.* New York: Kingfisher.

Caffey, D. (1998). *Yikes-lice!* Morton Grove, IL: Whitman.

Charlip, R. (1961). *Fortunately.* New York: Macmillan.

Clements, A. (1997). *Double trouble in Walla Walla.* Brookfield, CT: Millbrook Press.

Clifton, L. (1969). *Good times.* New York: Random House.

Clifton, L. (1970). *Some of the days of Everett Anderson.* New York: Holt.

Clifton, L. (1974). *The times they used to be.* New York: Holt.

Farber, N. (1973). *I found them in the yellow pages.* Boston: Little, Brown.

George, K.O. (1998). *Old elm speaks: Tree poems.* New York: Clarion.

Gwynne, F. (1976). *A chocolate moose for dinner.* Englewood Cliffs, NJ: Prentice Hall.

Gwynne, F. (1980). *The sixteen hand horse.* New York: Simon & Schuster.

Gwynne, F. (1988). *The king who rained.* New York: Simon & Schuster.

Heller, R. (1987). *A cache of jewels and other collective nouns.* New York: Grossett & Dunlap.

Heller, R. (1988). *Kites sail high: A book about verbs.* New York: Grossett & Dunlap.

Heller, R. (1989). *Many luscious lollipops: A book about adjectives.* New York: Grossett & Dunlap.

Heller, R. (1990). *Merry-go-round: A book about nouns.* New York: Grossett & Dunlap.

Heller, R. (1991). *Up, up and away: A book about adverbs.* New York: Grossett & Dunlap.

Heller, R. (1995). *Behind the mask: A book about prepositions.* New York: Grossett & Dunlap.

Heller, R. (1997). *Mine, all mine: A book about pronouns.* New York: Grosset & Dunlap.

Isaacs, A. (1998). *Cat up a tree.* New York: Dutton.

Joslin, S. (1962). *Dear Dragon...and other useful letter forms for young ladies and gentlemen engaged in everyday correspondence.* San Diego, CA: Harcourt Brace.

Kiralfy, B. (1997). *The most excellent book of how to be a cheerleader.* Brookfield, CT: Millbrook Press.

Larrick, N. (1988). *Cats are cats.* New York: Philomel.

Lewis, J.P. (1999). *The bookworm's feast: A potluck of poems.* New York: Dial.

Lewis, R. (1965). *In a spring garden.* New York: Dial.

MacDonald, F. (1998). *The stone age news.* Boston: Candlewick.

Martin, B. (1983). *Brown bear, brown bear, what do you see?* New York: Holt.

Morrison, T. (1999). *The big box.* New York: Hyperion.

Moss, M. (1998). *Amelia takes command.* Berkeley, CA: Tricycle Press.

O'Neill, A. (1998). *Loud Emily.* New York: Simon & Schuster.

O'Neill, M. (1966). *What is that sound?* New York: Atheneum.

O'Neill, M. (1969). *Fingers are always bringing me news.* New York: Doubleday.

O'Neill, M. (1985). *Hailstones and halibut bones: Adventures in color* (2nd ed.). New York: Doubleday.

Parish, P. (1964). *Thank you, Amelia Bedelia.* New York: Harper.

Poole, A.L. (1999). *How the rooster got his crown.* New York: Holiday House.

Prelutsky, J. (1999). *The gargoyle on the roof.* New York: Greenwillow.

Rankin, J. (1997). *Wow! It's great being a duck.* New York: Simon & Schuster.

Reid, A. (1958). *Ounce dice trice.* Boston: Little, Brown.

Ringgold, F. (1995). *My dream of Martin Luther King.* New York: Crown.

Rylant, C. (1968). *Tikki tikki tembo.* New York: Scholastic.

Rylant, C. (1982). *When I was young in the mountains.* New York: Dutton.

Rylant, C. (1991). *Appalachia: The voices of sleeping birds.* San Diego, CA: Harcourt.

Rylant, C. (1992). *An angel for Solomon.* New York: Orchard Books.

Rylant, C. (1992). *Best wishes.* Katonah, NY: Richard C. Owen.

Rylant, C. (1992). *Missing May.* New York: Doubleday.

Rylant, C. (1997). *Margaret, Frank, and Andy: Three writers' stories.* San Diego, CA: Harcourt Brace.

Rylant, C. (1998). *Poppleton forever.* New York: Scholastic.

Rylant, C. (1998). *Tulip sees America.* New York: Scholastic.

Saul, C.P. (1998). *Barn cat.* Boston: Little, Brown.

Schimmel, S. (1994). *Dear children of the earth: A letter from home.* Minocqua, WI: North Word Press.

Schulz, C. (1963). *Happiness is a warm puppy.* San Francisco: Determined Press.

Spier, P. (1972). *Crash, bang, boom.* New York: Doubleday.

Sutherland, M. (1998). *The waiting place.* Waterbury, CT: Abrams.

Updike, J. (1995). *A helpful alphabet of friendly objects.* New York: Knopf.

Van Allsburg, C. (1984). *The mysteries of Harris Burdick.* Boston: Houghton Mifflin.

Viorst, J. (1972). *Alexander and his terrible, horrible, no good, very bad day.* New York: Atheneum.

Westcott, N.B. (1994). *Never take a pig to lunch and other poems about the fun of eating.* New York: Orchard Books.

Zindel, P. (1968). *The Pigman.* New York: Harper & Row.

Zindel, P. (1975). *I love my mother.* New York: Harper.

Zindel, P. (1999). *Reef of death.* New York: HarperCollins.

Zolotow, C. (1967). *All that sunlight.* New York: Harper.

Chapter 5

Ada, A.F. (1997). *Gathering the sun: An alphabet in Spanish and English.* New York: Lothrop, Lee & Shepard.

Brook, D. (1998). *The journey of English.* New York: Clarion.

Brown, M. (1961). *Once a mouse...A fable cut in wood.* New York: Scribner.

Browne, A. (1998). *Voices in the park.* New York: DK Publishing.

Burleigh, R. (1999). *Hercules.* San Diego, CA: Silver Whistle.

Charlip, R., & Beth, M. (1974). *Handtalk: An ABC of finger spelling & sign language.* New York: Scholastic.

Clayton, D.D. (1992). *The Adventures of Young Krishna: The blue god of India.* New York: Oxford University Press.

Contemporary Authors. Detroit, MI: Gale Research.

Cooney, B. (1958). *Chanticleer and the fox.* New York: Crowell.

Cooney, B. (1982). *Miss Rumphius.* New York: Viking.

Cornish, S. (1974). *Grandmother's pictures.* Bradbury.

Crews, D. (1991). *Bigmama's.* New York: Greenwillow.

DeRoin, N. (1975). *Jataka tales.* Boston: Houghton Mifflin.

Dickinson, E. (1978). *I'm nobody! Who are you?: Poems of Emily Dickinson for young people.* Owings Mills, MD: Stemmer House.

Garland, S. (1993). *The lotus seed.* San Diego, CA: Harcourt Brace.

Geography Department of Runestone Press. (1994). *Scrawl! Writing in ancient times.* Minneapolis, MN: Author.

Goldstein, P. (1991). *Long is a dragon: Chinese writing for children.* San Francisco, CA: China Books & Periodicals.

Grimm, J., & Grimm, W. (1979). *Hansel and Gretel* (E.D. Crawford, Trans.). New York: Morrow.

Heide, F. (1970). *Sound of sunshine, sound of rain.* Bowling Green, KY: Parents.

Holling, H.C. (1942). *Tree in the trail.* Boston: Houghton Mifflin.

Holling, H.C. (1957). *Pagoo.* Boston: Houghton Mifflin.

Holling, H.C. (1978). *Minn of the Mississippi.* Boston: Houghton Mifflin.

Hughes, L. (1994). *The dream keeper and other poems.* New York: Knopf.

Huygen, W. (1981). *Los gnomos.* Columbia: Intervisual Communications.

Jacobs, J. (1894). *The fables of Aesop.* New York: Macmillan.

Jones, H. (1971). *The trees stand shining: Poetry of the North American Indians.* New York: Dial.

Johnston, T. (1998). *Bigfoot Cinderrrrrella.* New York: Putnam.

Karas, G.B. (1998). *The windy day.* New York: Simon & Schuster.

Koch, K., & Farrell, K. (1985). *Talking to the sun: An illustrated anthology of poems for young people.* New York: Metropolitan Museum of Art and Henry Holt and Company.

Krishnaswami, U. (1996). *The broken tusk: Stories of the Hindu god Ganesha.* North Haven, CT: Linnet Books.

Loewen, N. (1999). *Hercules.* Mankato, MN: River Front.

Loewen, N. (1999). *Athena.* Mankato, MN: River Front.

McDermott, G. (1984). *Daughter of Earth: A Roman myth.* New York: Delacorte.

Merriam, E. (1960). *A gaggle of geese.* New York: Knopf.

Merriam, E. (1969). *The inner city Mother Goose.* New York: Simon & Schuster.

Minters, F. (1994). *Cinder-Elly.* New York: Viking.

Newman, R. (1972). *The twelve labors of Hercules.* New York: Crowell.

Nickl, P. (1985). *The story of the kind wolf.* (M. Koenig, Trans.). New York: North-South Books.

Nye, N. (1995). *The tree is older than you are: A bilingual gathering of poems and stories from Mexico.* New York: Simon & Schuster.

Pinkney, G.J. (1992). *Back home.* New York: Dial.

Riordan, J. (1997). *The twelve labors of Hercules.* Brookfield, CT: Millbrook Press.

Rockwell, A.F. (1997). *Romulus and Remus.* New York: Simon & Schuster.

Rossner, J. (1973). *What kind of feet does a bear have?* Englewood Cliffs, NJ: Merrill.

Sathre, V. (1999). *Slender Ella and her fairy hogfather.* New York: Delacorte.

Shepard, A. (1992). *Savitri: A tale of ancient India.* Morton Grove, IL: Whitman.

Shulevitz, U. (1974). *Dawn.* New York: Farrar, Straus & Giroux.

Scieszka, J. (1989). *The true story of the 3 little pigs by A. Wolf.* New York: Viking.

Scieszka, J. (1998). *Squids will be squids.* New York: Viking.

Talbott, H. (1991). *King Arthur: The sword in the stone.* New York: Morrow.

Talbott, H. (1995). *King Arthur and the round table.* New York: Morrow.

Talbott, H. (1996). *Excalibur.* New York: Morrow.

Talbott, H. (1999). *Lancelot: Tales of King Arthur.* New York: Morrow.

Thomas, J.C. (1993). *Brown honey in broomwheat tea.* New York: HarperCollins.

Whipple, L. (1994). *Celebrating America: A collection of poems and images of the American spirit.* New York: Philomel.

Wyeth, S.D. (1998). *Something beautiful.* New York: Doubleday.

Chapter 6

Ackerman, K. (1988). *Song and dance man.* New York: Scholastic.

Ada, A.F. (1998). *The malachite palace.* New York: Simon & Schuster.

Archambault, J. (1997). *Grandmother's garden.* New York: Simon & Schuster.

Bang, M. (1999). *When Sophie gets angry—really, really angry.* New York: Scholastic.

Belloc, H. (1991). *Matilda, who told lies, and was burned to death.* New York: Knopf.

Bloom, B. (1999). *Wolf!* New York: Orchard Books.

Bodecker, N.M. (1998). *Hurry, hurry, Mary dear.* New York: Simon & Schuster.

Browne, A. (1984). *Willy the wimp.* New York: Knopf.

Bunting, E. (1989). *The Wednesday surprise.* New York: Clarion.

Bunting, E. (1994). *Smoky night.* San Diego, CA: Harcourt Brace.

Bunting, E. (1998). *So far from the sea.* New York: Clarion.

Clifton, L. (1976). *Everett Anderson's friend.* New York: Holt.

Coles, R. (1995). *The story of Ruby Bridges.* New York: Scholastic.

Cutler, J. (1999). *The cello of Mr. O.* New York: Dutton.

David, A. (1982). *A picture book of Hanukkah.* New York: Holiday House.

Ehrlich, A. (1989). *The story of Hanukkah.* New York: Dial.

Farber, N. (1979). *How does it feel to be old?* New York: Dutton.

Fleming, C. (1999). *When Agnes caws.* New York: Atheneum.

Fox, M. (1985). *Wilfrid Gordon McDonald Partridge.* Brooklyn, NY: Kane/Miller.

Goble, P. (1998). *The legend of the white buffalo woman.* Washington, DC: National Geographic Society.

Greenfield, E. (1974). *She come bringing me that little baby girl.* New York: Lippincott.

Hansen, J. (1998). *Women of hope: African Americans who made a difference.* New York: Scholastic.

Henkes, K. (1993). *Owen.* New York: Greenwillow.

Hildebrandt, Z. (1999). *This is our Seder.* New York: Holiday House.

Hirsh, M. (1973). *Ben goes into business.* New York: Holiday House.

Hobbs, W. (1998). *Howling hill.* New York: Morrow.

Hoffman, M. (1991). *Amazing Grace.* New York: Dial.

Jimenez, F. (1998). *La mariposa.* Boston: Houghton Mifflin.

Johnston, T. (1996). *The wagon.* New York: Morrow.

Keats, E.J. (1963). *The snowy day.* New York: Viking.

Kroeger, M.K., & Borden, L. (1996). *Paperboy.* New York: Clarion.

Leaf, M. (1939). *The story of Ferdinand.* New York: Viking.

Lionni, L. (1963). *Swimmy.* New York: Pantheon.

Livingstone, M.C. (Ed.). (1987). *I like you, if you like me: Poems of friendship.* New York: Margaret K. McElderry.

McKissack, P., & McKissack, F. (1994). *Christmas in the big house; Christmas in the quarters.* New York: Scholastic.

Mendez, P. (1989). *The black snowman.* New York: Scholastic.

Miller, W. (1994). *Zora Hurston and the chinaberry tree.* New York: Lee & Low.

Miller, W. (1997). *Richard Wright and the library card.* New York: Lee & Low.

Myers, W.D. (1997). *Amistad: A long road to freedom.* New York: Dutton.

Ness, E. (1966). *Sam, Bangs, and moonshine.* New York: Holt.

Paradis, S. (1998). *My daddy.* Asheville, NC: Front Street Books.

Phillips, M. (1985). *The sign on Mendel's window.* New York: Macmillan.

Podwal, M. (1998). *The menorah story.* New York: Greenwillow.

Polacco, P. (1992). *Chicken Sunday.* New York: Philomel.

Polacco, P. (1992). *Mrs. Katz and Tush.* New York: Dell.

Polacco, P. (1998). *Thank you, Mr. Falker.* New York: Philomel.

Radin, R.Y. (1991). *All Joseph wanted.* New York: Macmillan.

San Souci, R.D. (1989). *The talking eggs.* New York: Dial.

San Souci, R.D. (1999). *Brave Margaret: An Irish adventure.* New York: Simon & Schuster.

Schroeder, A. (1996). *Minty: A story of young Harriet Tubman.* New York: Dial.

Scieszka, J. (1989). *The true story of the 3 little pigs by A. Wolf.* New York: Viking.

Seuss, Dr. (1976). *The butter battle book.* New York: Random House.

Smalls, I. (1999). *Kevin and his dad.* Boston: Little, Brown.

Spinelli, E. (1998). *When Mama comes home tonight.* New York: Simon & Schuster.

Stanek, M. (1985). *I speak English for my mom.* New York: Whitman.

Steptoe, J. (1969). *Stevie*. New York: Harper.

Swinburne, S. (1999). *Once a wolf: How wildlife biologists fought to bring back the gray wolf*. Boston: Houghton Mifflin.

Turkle, B. (1972). *The adventures of Obadiah*. New York: Viking.

Uchida, Y. (1971). *Journey to Topaz*. New York: Scribner.

Uchida, Y. (1993). *The bracelet*. New York: Philomel.

Vozar, D. (1993). *Yo, hungry wolf!*. New York: Doubleday.

Waber, B. (1972). *Ira sleeps over*. Boston: Houghton Mifflin.

Walsh, E.S. (1998). *For Pete's sake*. San Diego, CA: Harcourt Brace.

Winter, J. (1988). *Follow the drinking gourd*. New York: Knopf.

Winthrop, E. (1998). *As the crow flies*. New York: Clarion.

Yarbrough, C. (1979). *Cornrows*. New York: Putnam.

Yashima, T. (1955). *Crow boy*. New York: Viking.

Yezerski, T.F. (1998). *Together in pinecone patch*. New York: Farrar, Straus & Giroux.

Zolotow, C. (1971). *A father like that*. New York: Harper.

Chapter 7

Adler, D. (1995). *A picture book of Paul Revere*. New York: Holiday House.

Ai-Ling, L. (1982). *Ieh-Shen: A Cinderella story from China*. New York: Philomel.

Alexander, L. (1992). *The fortune tellers*. New York: Dutton.

Anderson, J. (1993). *Earth keepers*. San Diego, CA: Harcourt Brace.

Anno, M., & Anno, M. (1983). *Anno's mysterious multiplying jar*. New York: Putnam.

Arnold, K. (1992). *Baba Yaga*. New York: North-South Books.

Babbit, N. (1998). *Ouch! A tale from Grimm*. New York: HarperCollins.

Brown, M. (1947). *Stone soup*. New York: Scribner.

Brown, M. (1955). *Cinderella: Or the little glass slipper*. New York: Scribner.

Blue, R., & Naden, C.J. (1997). *Colin Powell: Straight to the top*. Brookfield, CT: Millbrook Press.

Bunting, E. (2000). *Dreaming of America: An Ellis Island story*. Mahwah, NJ: Bridgewater Books.

Chambers, C. (1996). *Sikh*. San Francisco: Children's Book Press.

Clement, R. (1991). *Counting on Frank*. Milwaukee, WI: Garreth Stevens.

Climo, S. (1994). *The Egyptian Cinderella*. New York: HarperCollins.

Climo, S. (1993). *The Korean Cinderella*. New York: HarperCollins.

Climo, S. (1999). *The Persian Cinderella*. New York: HarperCollins.

Coburn, J.R., with Lee, T.C. (1997). *Jouanah: A Hmong Cinderella*. Arcadia, CA: Shen's Books.

Coburn, J.R. (1998). *Angkat, the Cambodian Cinderella*. Arcadia, CA: Shen's Books.

Coerr, E. (1993). *Sadako*. New York: Putnam.

Cohen, B. (1998). *Molly's Pilgrim*. New York: Lothrop, Lee & Shepard.

Cole, J. (1998). *The magic school bus in the rain forest*. New York: Scholastic.

Collay, R., & Dubrow, J. (1998). *Stuartship*. Eugene, OR: FlowerPress.

Cummings, P., & Cummings, L. (1998). *Talking with adventurers: Conversations with Christina M. Allen, Robert Ballard, Michael L. Blakey, Ann Bowles, David Doubilet, Jane Goodall, Dereck and Beverly Joubert, Michael Novacek, Johan Reinhard, Rick C. West, and Juris Zarins*. Washington, DC: National Geographic Society.

Demi. (1996). *Buddha*. New York: Holt.

Demi. (1997). *One grain of rice: A mathematical folktale*. New York: Scholastic.

Demi. (1999). *The donkey and the rock*. New York: Holt.

del Negro, J. (1998). *Lucy dove*. New York: DK Publishing.

Ehrlich, A. (1985). *Cinderella*. New York: Dial.

Facklam, M. (1989). *Do not disturb: The mysteries of animal hibernation and sleep*. Boston: Little, Brown.

Few, R. (1993). *Guide to endangered animals*. New York: Macmillan.

Fleming, D. (1992). *Count!* New York: Holt.

Forest, H. (1998). *Stone soup*. Little Rock, AR: August House.

Frasier, D. (1998). *Out of the ocean*. San Diego, CA: Harcourt Brace.

Fritz, J. (1994). *Harriet Beecher Stowe and the Beecher Preachers*. New York: Putnam.

Fritz, J. (1995). *You want women to vote, Lizzie Stanton?* New York: Putnam.

George, J.C. (1995). *Everglades*. New York: HarperCollins.

George, L.B. (1999). *Around the world: Who's been here?* New York: Greenwillow.

Gibbons, G. (1998). *Marshes & swamps*. New York: Holiday House.

Glass, A. (1995). *Folks call me Appleseed John*. New York: Doubleday.

Glass, J. (1998). *The fly on the ceiling: A math myth*. New York: Random House.

Glass, J. (1999). *A dollar for penny*. New York: Random House.

Goble, P. (1993). *Beyond the ridge*. New York: Aladdin.

Goble, P. (1999). *Iktomi loses his eyes*. New York: Orchard Books.

Goldsmith, D.H. (1996). *Day of the dead*. New York: Holiday House.

Graham, I., & Graham, A. (1998). *The best book of spaceships*. New York: Kingfisher.

Greenfield, E. (1974). *She come bringing me that little baby girl!* New York: Lippincott.

Greenfield, E. (1976). *Paul Robeson*. New York: Crowell.

Greenfield, E. (1977). *Mary McLeod Bethune*. New York: Crowell.

Grimes, N. (1999). *At break of day*. Grand Rapids, MI: Wm B Eerdmans.

Gukova, J. (1998). *The mole's daughter*. Toronto: Annick Press.

Hamilton, V. (1988). *In the beginning: Creation stories from around the world*. San Diego, CA: Harcourt Brace.

Hirschi, R. (1991). *Loon lake*. New York: Dutton.

Hoffman, M. (1997). *An angel just like me*. New York: Dial.

Holden, R. (1998). *The pied piper of Hamelin*. Boston: Houghton Mifflin.

Jaffe, N. (1998). *The way meat loves salt: A Cinderella tale from the Jewish tradition*. New York: Holt.

Keams, G. (1998). *Snail girl brings water: A Navajo story*. Flagstaff, AZ: Northland Publishing.

Kherdian, D. (1998). *The golden bracelet*. New York: Holiday House.

Kimmel, E.A. (1998). *Seven at a blow: A tale from the brothers Grimm*. New York: Holiday House.

Kimmel, E. (1999). *Ice story: Shackleton's lost expedition*. New York: Clarion.

Kirk, D. (1999). *Nova's ark*. New York: Scholastic.

Hickox, R. (1999). *The golden sandal: A Middle Eastern Cinderella story*. New York: Holiday House.

Knight, M.B. (1992). *Talking walls*. Gardiner, ME: Tilbury House.

Knight, M.B. (1996). *Talking walls: The stories continue*. Gardiner, ME: Tilbury House.

Kraft, B.H. (1995). *Mother Jones: One woman's fight for labor*. New York: Clarion.

Lee, C.C. (1997). *A is for Asia*. New York: Orchard Books.

Lee, C.C., & de la Pena, T. (1999). *A is for the Americas*. New York: Orchard Books.

Lester, J. (1999). *What a truly cool world*. New York: Scholastic.

Lester, J. (1999). *When the beginning began*. San Diego, CA: Harcourt Brace.

Maestro, B. (1997). *The story of religion*. New York: Clarion.

Maynard, T. (1993). *Saving endangered birds: Ensuring a future in the wild*. Danbury, CT: Watts.

McKissack, P., & McKissack, F. (1998). *Let my people go: Bible stories told by a freeman of color*. New York: Atheneum.

Milord, S. (1995). *Tales alive: Ten multicultural folktales with activities*. Charlotte, VT: Williamson Publishing.

Murphy, S.J. (1997). *Betcha!* New York: HarperCollins.

Nye, N.S. (1998). *The space between our footsteps: Poems and paintings from the Middle East*. New York: Simon & Schuster.

Perrault, C. (1967). *Perrault's classic French fairy tales*. New York: Meredith.

Perrault, C. (1989). *Cinderella and other tales from Perrault*. New York: Holt.

Petty, K. (1997). *I didn't know that dinosaurs laid eggs*. Brookfield, CT: Millbrook Press.

Platt, R. (1992). *Stephen Biesty's incredible cross-sections*. New York: DK Publishing.

Platt, R. (1993). *Stephen Biesty's cross-sections man-of-war*. New York: DK Publishing.

Platt, R. (1994). *Stephen Biesty's cross-sections castle*. New York: DK Publishing.

Platt, R. (1996). *Stephen Biesty's incredible explosions*. New York: DK Publishing.

Platt, R. (1997). *Stephen Biesty's incredible everything*. New York: DK Publishing.

Platt, R. (1998). *Stephen Biesty's incredible body*. New York: DK Publishing.

Prose, F. (1998). *You never know: A legend of the lamed-vavniks*. New York: Greenwillow.

Reynolds, D.W. (1999). *Star Wars Episode I: The visual dictionary*. New York: DK Publishing.

Richards, J. (1998). *Cutaway train*. Brookfield, CT: Millbrook Press.

Rosen, M.J. (1992). *Elijah's angel*. San Diego, CA: Harcourt Brace.

Roth, S.L. (1994). *Buddha*. New York: Doubleday.

Rothmann, E. (1994). *Time flies*. New York: Crown.

Russell, S.P. (1970). *Peanuts, popcorn, ice cream, candy, and soda pop and how they began*. Nashville, TN: Abingdon Press.

San Souci, R.D. (1994). *Sootface: An Ojibwa Cinderella story*. New York: Doubleday.

San Souci, R.D. (1995). *The faithful friend*. New York: Simon & Schuster.

San Souci, R.D. (1998). *Cendrillon: A Caribbean Cinderella*. New York: Simon & Schuster.

Say, A. (1993). *Grandfather's journey*. Boston: Houghton Mifflin.

Schachner, J. (1998). *Mr. Emerson's cook*. New York: Dutton.

Schlein, M. (1996). *More than one*. New York: Greenwillow.

Schwartz, D. (1985). *How much is a million?* New York: Lothrop, Lee & Shepard.

Schwartz, D. (1989). *If you made a million*. New York: Lothrop, Lee & Shepard.

Schwartz, D. (1998). *G is for googol*. Berkeley, CA: Tricycle Press.

Schwartz, D. (1999). *On beyond a million*. New York: Bantam.

Scott, M. (1995). *The young Oxford book of ecology*. New York: Oxford University Press.

Seuss, Dr. (1990). *The 500 hats of Bartholomew Cubbins*. New York: Random House.

Silverman, E. (1997). *The Halloween house*. New York: Farrar, Straus & Giroux.

Silverman, E. (1999). *Raisel's riddle*. New York: Farrar, Straus & Giroux.

Simon, N. (1987). *Vanishing habitats*. New York: Gloucester Press.

Sís, P. (1990). *Starry messenger: A book depicting the life of a famous scientist, mathematician, astronomer, philosopher, and physicist, Galileo Galilei*. New York: Farrar, Straus & Giroux.

Small, E. (1966). *Baba Yaga*. Boston: Houghton Mifflin.

Spier, P. (1977). *Noah's ark*. New York: Delacorte.

Stanley, D. (1997). *Rumplestiltskin's daughter*. New York: Morrow.

Steptoe, J. (1987). *Mufaro's beautiful daughters*. New York: Lothrop, Lee & Shepard.

Sterne, N. (1979). *Tyrannosaurus wrecks: A book of dinosaur riddles*. New York: Crowell.

Tolstoy, A., & Sharkey. (1998). *The gigantic turnip*. Brooklyn, NY: Barefoot Books.

Tsuchiya, Y. (1988). *Faithful elephants: A true story of animals, people, and war*. Boston: Houghton Mifflin.

VanCleave, J. (1996). *Ecology for every kid: Easy activities that make learning science fun*. New York: Wiley.

Wildsmith, B. (1965). *Brian Wildsmith's 1,2,3's*. Danbury, CT: Watts.

Yamaguchi, K., with Brown, G. (1998). *Always dream*. Dallas, TX: Taylor Publishing.

Yolen, J. (1996). *O Jerusalem*. St. Paul, MN: Blue Sky Press.

Chapter 8

Aardema, V. (1976). *Why mosquitoes buzz in people's ears*. New York: Dial.

Ada, A.F. (1997). *Gathering the sun: An alphabet in Spanish and English*. New York: Lothrop, Lee & Shepard.

Barnwell, Y.M. (1998). *No mirrors in my nana's house*. San Diego, CA: Harcourt Brace.

Baylor, B. (1976). *The desert is theirs*. New York: Scribner.

Blackstone, S. (1997). *Baby high, baby low*. New York: Holiday House.

Bornstein, R. (1998). *The dancing man*. New York: Clarion.

Bourke, L. (1991). *Eye spy: A mysterious alphabet*. New York: Chronicle Books.

Chandra, D. (1999). *A is for Amos*. New York: Farrar, Straus & Giroux.

Craft, M.C. (1996). *Cupid and psyche*. New York: Morrow.

Cummings, P. (1992). *Talking with artists*. New York: Bradbury.

Curtis, G. (1998). *The bat boy & his violin*. New York: Simon & Schuster.

Cutler, J. (1999). *The cello of Mr. O.* New York: Dutton.

Demi. (1999). *The donkey and the rock.* New York: Holt.

dePaola, T. (1975). *Strega Nona.* New York: Simon & Schuster.

dePaola, T. (1984). *Mary had a little lamb.* New York: Holiday House.

dePaola, T. (1985). *Tomie dePaola's Mother Goose.* New York: Putnam.

dePaola, T. (1998). *Nana upstairs & Nana downstairs* (Rev. ed.). New York: Putnam.

dePaola, T. (1999). *The night of las posadas.* New York: Putnam.

Dillon, L., & Dillon, D. (1998). *To every thing there is a season.* New York: Scholastic.

Duggleday, J. (1995). *Artist in overalls: The life of Grant Wood.* New York: Chronicle Books.

Edwards, P. (1998). *Honk!* New York: Hyperion.

Elleman, B. (1999). *Tomie dePaola: His art and his stories.* New York: Putnam.

Emberly, B. (1968). *Drummer Hoff.* Englewood Cliffs, NJ: Prentice Hall.

Engel, D., & Freedman, F.B. (1995). *Ezra Jack Keats: A biography with illustrations.* New York: Silver Moon Press.

Frasier, D. (1998). *Out of the ocean.* San Diego, CA: Harcourt Brace.

Gabler, M. (1992). *The alphabet soup.* New York: Holt.

Goldsmith, D.H., & Migdale, L. (1999). *Las posadas: An Hispanic Christmas celebration.* New York: Holiday House.

Goldstone, B. (1998). *The beastly feast.* New York: Holt.

Gray, L.M. (1995). *My mama had a dancing heart.* New York: Orchard Books.

Guthrie, W. (1998). *This land is your land.* Boston: Little, Brown.

Harrison, T. (1982). *A northern alphabet.* Plattsburgh, NY: Tundra Books.

Helprin, M. (1989). *Swan lake.* Boston: Houghton Mifflin.

Hepworth, C. (1992). *ANTICS! An alphabetical anthology.* New York: Putnam.

Hughes, L. (1994). *The sweet and sour animal book.* New York: Oxford University Press.

Hunt, J. (1989). *Illuminations.* New York: Macmillan.

Johnson, S. (1995). *Alphabet city.* New York: Viking.

Jordan, T. (1993). *Jungle days, jungle nights.* New York: Kingfisher.

Jordan, T. (1995). *Angel falls: A South American journey.* New York: Kingfisher.

Jordan, T. (1996). *Amazon alphabet.* New York: Kingfisher.

Keats, E.J. (1962). *The snowy day.* New York: Viking.

Keats, E.J. (1964). *Whistle for Willie.* New York: Viking.

Keats, E.J. (1967). *Peter's chair.* New York: Viking.

Keeping, C. (1969). *In Joseph's yard.* Danbury, CT: Watts.

Kellogg, S. (1987). *Aster Aardvark's alphabet adventures.* New York: Morrow.

Kiesler, K. (1999). *Ocean lullabies and night verses.* New York: Clarion.

King, M.L. (1997). *I have a dream.* New York: Scholastic.

Lawrence, J. (1993). *The great migration.* New York: Museum of Modern Art, HarperCollins.

Lear, E. (1998). *The owl and the pussy cat.* New York: HarperCollins.

Lobel, A. (1981). *On Market Street.* New York: Greenwillow.

Lobel, A. (1990). *Alison's zinnia*. New York: Greenwillow.

Locker, T. (1987). *The boy who held back the sea*. New York: Dial.

Lottridge, C.B. (1998). *Music of the tsar of the sea*. New York: Douglas & McIntyre.

Mayer, M. (1982). *The unicorn and the lake*. New York: Dial.

Mayer, M. (1989). *The unicorn alphabet*. New York: Dial

McDermott, G. (1974). *Arrow to the sun: A Pueblo Indian tale*. New York: Viking.

Metaxas. E. (1995). *The birthday ABC*. New York: Simon & Schuster.

Moore, C.C. (1980). *The night before Christmas*. New York: Holiday House.

Musgrove, M. (1976). *Ashanti to Zulu: African traditions*. New York: Dial.

Ness, E. (1967). *Sam, Bangs, and moonshine*. New York: Holt.

Newfeld, F. (1998). *Creatures: An alphabet for adults and worldly children*. New York: Douglas & McIntyre.

Owens, M.B. (1988). *A Caribou alphabet*. Middleton, WI: Dog-Eared Press.

Pinkney, A.D. (1993). *Alvin Ailey*. New York: Hyperion.

Poindexter, K. (1998). *Disney's Mulan*. New York: Golden Books.

Presilla, M.E. (1996). *Mola: Cuna life, stories and art*. New York: Holt.

Provensen, A., & Provensen, M. (1987). *Shaker lane*. New York: Puffin.

Ringgold, F. (1991). *Tar beach*. New York: Crown.

Ringgold, F. (1992). *Aunt Harriet's underground railroad in the sky*. New York: Crown.

Rochelle, B. (1998). *Jewels*. New York: Lodestar.

San Souci, R.D. (1986). *The legend of Sleepy Hollow*. New York: Doubleday.

San Souci, R.D. (1998). *Cendrillon: A Caribbean Cinderella*. New York: Simon & Schuster.

San Souci, R.D. (1998). *Fa Mulan: The story of a woman warrior*. New York: Hyperion.

Saport, L. (1999). *All the pretty little horses*. New York: Clarion.

Schenk de Regniers, B. (1965). *May I bring a friend?* New York: Atheneum.

Schrier, J. (1998). *On the wings of eagles: An Ethiopian boy's story*. Brookfield, CT: Millbrook Press.

Sendak, M. (1963). *Where the wild things are*. New York: Harper.

Sendak, M. (1988). *Dear Mili*. New York: Farrar, Straus & Giroux.

Shulevitz, U. (1998). *Snow*. New York: Farrar, Straus & Giroux.

Steiner, T.J. (1998). *A bug's life: Classic storybook*. New York: Mouseworks (Disney/Pixar).

Steptoe, J. (1969). *Stevie*. New York: Harper.

Story, T. (1989). *Glenn Close reads the legend of Sleepy Hollow*. New York: Rabbit Ears.

Tames, T. (1991). *Frederic Chopin*. Danbury, CT: Watts.

Tapahonso, L., & Schick, E. (1995). *Navajo ABC: A Dine alphabet book*. New York: Simon & Schuster.

Turner, R.M. (1993). *Faith Ringgold*. Boston: Little, Brown.

Vernon, R. (1996). *Introducing Gershwin*. Parsippany, NJ: Silver Burdett Ginn.

Viorst, J. (1994). *The alphabet from Z to A (with much confusion on the way)*. New York: Atheneum.

Wallner, A. (1998). *The farmer in the dell*. New York: Holiday House.

Wells, R. (1992). *A to Zen: A book of Japanese culture*. New York: Simon & Schuster.

Westcott, N.B. (1980). *I know an old lady who swallowed a fly*. Boston: Little, Brown.

Winter, J. (1998). *My name is Georgia: A portrait*. San Diego, CA: Harcourt Brace.

Winter, J. (1999). *Sebastian: A book about Bach*. San Diego, CA: Harcourt Brace.

Ziefert, H. (1999). *Animal music*. Boston: Houghton Mifflin.

Zoehfeld, K.W. (1998). *Disney's Mulan*. New York: Disney Enterprises.

Chapter 9

Aliki. (1998). *Marianthe's story: Painted words, spoken memories*. New York: Greenwillow.

Atkins, J. (1999). *A name on the quilt: A story of remembrance*. New York: Atheneum.

Baylor, B. (1986). *I'm in charge of celebrations*. New York: Scribner.

Best, C. (1999). *Three cheers for Catherine the great!* New York: DK Publishing.

Bial, R. (1996). *With needle and thread: A book about quilts*. Boston: Houghton Mifflin.

Booth, B., & Lamarche, J. (1991). *Mandy*. New York: Lothrop, Lee & Shepard.

Bruchac, J., & London, J. (1992). *Thirteen moons on turtle's back: A Native American year of moons*. New York: Philomel.

Bunting, E. (1988). *How many days to America?: A Thanksgiving story*. New York: Clarion.

Bunting, E. (1994). *Smoky night*. San Diego, CA: Harcourt Brace.

Capote, T. (1989). *A Christmas memory*. New York: Knopf.

Carter, D. (1998). *Bye, Mis' Lela*. New York: Farrar, Straus & Giroux.

Cobb, M. (1995). *The quilt block history of pioneer days*. Brookfield, CT: Millbrook Press.

Coerr, E. (1989). *The Josefina story quilt*. New York: Harper.

Cole, J., with Saul, W. (1996). *On the bus with Joanna Cole: A creative autobiography*. Portsmouth, NH: Heinemann.

Cooney, B. (1982). *Miss Rumphius*. New York: Viking.

Crews, D. (1991). *Bigmama's*. New York: Greenwillow.

Dale, E. (1998). *How long?* New York: Orchard Books.

DeGross, M. (1999). *Granddaddy's street songs*. New York: Hyperion.

Dorros, A. (1991). *Abuela*. New York: Dutton.

Dungworth, R. (1997). *The Usborne book of famous women*. London: Usborne.

Flournoy, V. (1985). *The patchwork quilt*. New York: Dial.

Ford, M. (1998). *Mom and me*. New York: Greenwillow.

Fox, M. (1989). *Wilfred Gordon McDonald Partridge*. Brooklyn, NY: Kane/Miller.

Freedman, R. (1980). *Immigrant kids*. New York: Dutton.

Goble, P. (1998). *The legend of the white buffalo woman*. Washington, DC: National Geographic Society.

Heide, F. (1969). *Sound of sunshine, sound of rain*. Bowling Green, KY.

Holling, H.C. (1942). *Tree in the trail*. Boston: Houghton Mifflin.

Hopkinson, D. (1993). *Sweet Clara and the freedom quilt*. New York: Knopf.

Howard, E. (1989). *The log cabin quilt*. New York: Harper.

Joosse, B.M. (1996). *I love you the purplest.* New York: Chronicle Books.

Levine, J.G. (1975). *A bedtime story.* New York: Dutton.

Levinson, R. (1985). *Watch the stars come out.* New York: Penguin.

Levinson, R. (1993). *Soon, Annala.* New York: Orchard Books.

Martin, J.B. (1998). *Snowflake Bentley.* Boston: Houghton Mifflin.

McDermott, G. (1993). *Raven: A trickster tale from the Pacific Northwest.* San Diego, CA: Harcourt Brace.

McPhail, D. (1997). *In flight with David McPhail: A creative autobiography.* Portsmouth, NH: Heinemann.

Miller, W. (1994). *Zora Hurston and the chinaberry tree.* New York: Lee & Low.

Morrison, T., & Morrison, S. (1999). *The big box.* New York: Hyperion.

Moss, M. (1999). *The all-new Amelia.* Middleton, WI: Pleasant Company.

O'Kelley, M.L. (1983). *From the hills of Georgia: An autobiography in paintings.* Boston: Little, Brown.

Parin d'Aulaire, I., & Parin d'Aulaire, E. (1962). *Book of Greek Myths.* New York: Doubleday.

Parin d'Aulaire, I., & Parin d'Aulaire, E. (1967). *Norse gods and giants.* New York: Doubleday.

Pinkney, G.J. (1992). *Back home.* New York: Dial.

Polacco, P. (1988). *The keeping quilt.* New York: Simon & Schuster.

Polacco, P. (1992). *Mrs. Katz and Tush.* New York: Dell.

Ringgold, R. (1991). *Tar beach.* New York: Crown.

Rylant, C. (1982). *When I was young on the mountain.* New York: Dutton.

Schroeder, A. (1996). *Minty: A story of young Harriet Tubman.* New York: Dial.

Shepard, A. (1992). *Savitri: A tale of ancient India.* New York: Whitman.

Silverstein, S. (1964). *The giving tree.* New York: Harper.

Steig, W. (1989). *Sylvester and the magic pebble.* New York: Scholastic.

Torres, L. (1998). *Liliana's grandmothers.* New York: Farrar, Straus & Giroux.

Van Camp, R. (1998). *What's the most beautiful thing you know about horses?* San Francisco: Children's Book Press.

Waddell, M. (1999). *Who do you love?* Boston: Candlewick.

Ziefert, H. (1998). *When I first came to this land.* New York: Putnam.

Zindel, P. (1975). *I love my mother.* New York: Harper.

INDEX

A

F

G

H

N

O

P–Q